99 THINGS TO DO Before You Finish High School

Revised and Updated

Text copyright © 2026 by Lerner Publishing Group, Inc.
Illustrations © 2007 by Azadeh Houshyar

All rights reserved. No part of this book may be reproduced, stored in a retrieval system, or transmitted in any form or by any means—electronic, mechanical, photocopying, recording, or otherwise—without the prior written permission of Lerner Publishing Group, Inc., except for the inclusion of brief quotations in an acknowledged review.

Zest Books™
An imprint of Lerner Publishing Group, Inc.
241 First Avenue North
Minneapolis, MN 55401 USA

For reading levels and more information, look up this title at www.lernerbooks.com.
Visit us at zestbooks.net.

Design elements: Farah Sadikhova/Shutterstock.
Cover: ZillaDigital/Shutterstock (plaid pattern).

Main body text set in Sabon LT Std.
Typeface provided by Adobe Systems.

Library of Congress Cataloging-in-Publication Data

The Cataloging-in-Publication Data for *99 Things to Do Before You Finish High School (Revised and Updated)* is on file at the Library of Congress.
ISBN 979-8-3480-2510-6 (lib. bdg.)
ISBN 979-8-3480-2511-3 (pbk.)
ISBN 979-8-3480-2764-3 (epub)

Manufactured in the United States of America
1-1012834-58622-8/27/2025

Revised and Updated

99 Things to Do Before You Finish High School

Steve Jenkins,
Erika Stalder,
and Evan Villas
with art by
Azadeh Houshyar

ZEST BOOKS
MINNEAPOLIS

99 Things to Do . . .

Part 1: For Your Personal Development

Part 2: With/For Friends

99 Things to Do . . .

Part 3: With/For Family

Part 4: For Your Body

Part 5: To Get to Know the World Around You

Part 6: To Express Yourself

Part 7: For Your Community and Environment

Part 8: Because You Should

Part 9: Because You're Only Young Once

This is the best time of your life—

or so people keep telling you.

But then, those same people tell you to clean your room, be home before ten, work on the weekends, and hand in twenty-page research papers. Uh, okay.

Whether or not *you* think this is the best time of your life (and the truth is, for most people, it keeps getting better), it *is* a unique time. As a teenager, you have the capacity to learn anything you want at a speed much faster than people who are only five years older, and your curiosity and insightfulness are at an all-time high.

So, what to do with this valuable time? Well, you can't stop doing the things you have to do. School, home, family: These are all aspects of basic life maintenance. But how you spend your free time—now, that's a different story. In this book, you'll learn things nobody teaches you in class, like how to throw a party, take a road trip, and live through the social media age. You'll also learn how to do your part to protect the environment, help out around your community, and express yourself in all sorts of ways.

There's a lot in here, and you certainly don't have to do it *all*. Pick what speaks to you. Go chronologically or flip through. Most important, use it to get ideas about how you want to spend your time and who you want to be. Because, as the cliché goes, you're only young once. And it just happens to be now.

1 Redo Your Bedroom

Your bedroom—or your section of a shared bedroom—may be the only space you can really call your own. But who chose the furniture, the wallpaper, the paint? A parent? A younger version of you? Might be time to redecorate! Even if you don't have the time, patience, or cash for a complete overhaul, you can transform your space to make it unmistakably yours.

How to Do It

Get permission. Clear your vision with parental authorities. (It may be *your* room, but it's technically contained in *their* home.) If you live in a rented home, you may need to check with your landlord before making significant changes, like painting or putting holes in the walls. If you share a room with someone, you may be able to collaborate or compromise. If not, focus on personalizing your part of the space while respecting their territory.

Clean up. Tidying your room can help you see exactly how much space you have to work with and inspire you to use that space effectively. Sort through the junk you've accumulated over the years and really think about what you want or don't want to keep in your reimagined room.

PAINTING SUPPLIES

Here's what you'll need for wall painting:

- **Paint.** A gallon (3.8 L) is enough for about one coat of 250 square feet (23 sq. m).
- **Spackle.** You can use this to fill cracks or holes in the wall.
- **Primer.** You'll need a base coat if you're covering a dark color with a light color.
- **Rollers.** Get short ones for the walls and longer ones (or an attachable extension) if you plan to paint the ceiling.
- **Paint trays.** You probably don't want to pour your paint on the floor!
- **Paintbrushes.** Get a variety of sizes—bigger, flat-tipped ones for walls and smaller, angle-tipped ones for trim.
- **Drop cloths.** Plastic is cheaper; canvas is sturdier. Better to buy too many than too few. Without proper coverage, that's the end of your floor.
- **Painter's tape.** Use this to secure drop cloths and put a protective border around windows, ceiling fixtures, and wall outlets. Also have some rags on hand to wipe up rogue splatters.
- **Small plastic containers.** Pour paint into these so you don't have to dip brushes directly into the can.

Paint. Measure the square footage of your space and get supplies from a paint store or hardware store. Choose a color depending on the mood you're going for: Vibrant colors will brighten your space; pastels will create a relaxed environment. Are you a budding artist? Slap on a soft white and turn your walls into a canvas. The entire job should take two days tops.

Add flair. Once the paint's dry, think about what else you'd like to look at every day. Plaster your walls with posters of your favorite band or sports team. Fill a shelf with your YA novels or tabletop RPG figurines.

Find new furniture. Check thrift stores or Facebook Marketplace for marked-down bookcases, tables, and odds and ends. Some people give away old furniture for free if you can pick it up yourself.

Clear the clutter. Donate, sell, recycle, or responsibly throw away whatever you can't use.

2 Start a Collection

Collections can be a cool way to show off your personality if they're thoughtfully maintained. Of course, if certain items increase in value as time goes by, they can turn into an excellent investment. Rare Pokémon cards sell for hundreds if not thousands of dollars every day. Classic Barbie dolls pull in hundreds. But collecting isn't about money. It's about surrounding yourself with things you love. Whether you're into baseball cards, vintage snow globes, or limited-edition Legos, starting a collection will send you on a rewarding quest that will never need to be completed. The fun is in the process.

How to Do It

Survey your possessions. If you have three or more of a certain type of object, you already have the makings of a collection! What about a drawer filled with classic Hello Kitty stationery or that box full of *Magic: The Gathering* cards? It doesn't have to be something expensive, valuable, or even rare, as long as it feels distinctive and meaningful to you.

Choose what you'll use. Focus on something you love that's accessible, affordable, and enjoyable to have around. Mint-condition LPs from legendary indie labels like Rawkus Records or Sub Pop will feed your music fix *and* look great framed and hung on the wall. Retro video game accessories and vintage jeans are as functional as they are quirky. Same goes for items from nature—for instance, abalone shells that can double as jewelry holders.

Be selective. Consider how much space you have to work with. You don't want to gather a ton of musical instruments and then realize you have no room to store them. (Jack White famously removed the bed from his childhood room to make room for more instruments—not a practical move for most of us!) Set limits on yourself so that your collection doesn't get out of control. For instance, allot one drawer, one reasonably sized box, one wall of your room, or X amount of money. If you find yourself breaching containment, cull a few of your least favorite items from the mix.

ONLINE BUYING

Online auctioning sites like eBay are hubs for buying and selling high-value collectibles. Facebook Marketplace will show you folks in your area who are selling items. Check both of these regularly, as highly collectible items are scooped up quickly.

3 Create a Journal

Take a little time each day to record what's going on in your life. This can be a great way to process your feelings, from venting frustration to sorting through confusion. The best part about journaling is that you don't have to edit your thoughts to please others. Granted, there may be plenty going on these days that you'd rather forget than remember, but your future self will be glad you recorded high school–era high points and horrors for posterity. Even something small—the joke your friend told you in class, the poor excuse for food that grouchy cafeteria worker slapped on your tray—may seem poignant or hilarious when you read about it years from now.

How to Do It

Choose a format. You can use a physical notebook or a journaling app.

Set your own schedule. You can add entries whenever you like. There are no rules to follow. You might decide to write a little every day after school or before bed. Or you might wait until the weekend. You might skip a few days or weeks and then pour your heart out when you're hit with big feelings.

Write what you want. You can record long recaps of your day or just make lists of things that drive you up the wall. Draft poems or confess crushes. Confess your little (and not so little) white lies. Whatever you need to get off your chest, your journal will never judge you.

Keep it safe. To protect these private thoughts, keep your journal away from prying eyes. Store a physical book somewhere nobody else will stumble onto it. If your journal is online, limit its access with a unique password that no one would be able to guess.

EXPLORING THE BLOGOSPHERE

Do you have thoughts you can't bear to keep to yourself? It's normal to want to share your ideas. If you have more to say than the Instagram character limit allows, you might want to start your own blog. Blogging sites make it easy to set up an account and get writing. Some let you customize your blog's web page for a small fee. Tumblr can also work as a quasi-blog/social media page with built-in tools to help you find an audience for your musings. Of course, there's a downside: Privacy is pretty much out the window. Make sure you don't reveal anything too personal online. If you don't want your mom or a future employer reading it, you probably shouldn't post it—because you never know who may find it someday. Keep identifying information, such as where you live and go to school, to an absolute minimum, and stay vigilant for shady activity on your page.

4 Assemble a Photo Album

You probably have thousands of photos on your phone: documentation of everything from dysfunctional family trips to out-of-control birthday parties to your younger sister's sorry attempt to cut her bangs. These photos can be so much more than fodder for your next carefully constructed Instagram photo dump. The internet is forever—until your favorite social media app shuts down, gets paywalled, or gets weird. It never hurts to have a physical backup of anything with sentimental value. That's where real, physical photo albums come in handy. You can carry them with you and tell stories about your (mis)adventures without having to pass around a tiny screen or log in to a site you haven't used in three years. Organize your camera roll and decide which moments are most worth remembering.

How to Do It

Get prints. To release your photos from the confines of your phone, upload them to a photo website that will print and mail them to you. Your local chain pharmacy might let you upload photos from your mobile device and print them out in the store.

Organize. Choose pics that cover a specific time frame (last summer), event (prom), or group of friends and select the photos you want to print. Buy a photo album online or at the store. The simplest ones have plastic sleeves you can pop the photos into. Or you can get the kind with blank pages and insert photos into those little black corner adhesives—this style is better for adding captions.

Design. Artfully arrange the photos to convey the story you want to tell. Capture the whimsy of last summer's family camping trip or the horrors of four straight 100°F (38°C) days at band camp. Spending time with these photos is a great way to relive the events you're chronicling and reflect on the good ol' times.

LAST-MINUTE PRESENT

Forgot to get a gift in time for Mother's Day, your good friend's birthday, or your cousin's quinceañera? Give them a card letting them know their gift is being custom made. Then photograph the event and assemble the photo album afterward. You can quickly create an album online through most photo sites and have it shipped directly to the recipient as a complete book. When taking pictures, be sure to capture more than just the people—details like the giant chocolate cake, the over-the-top flower arrangements, or the dog's unexpected splash into the pool will help capture the feeling of the entire event and make your album an irreplaceable gift.

5 Listen to New Music

When it comes to music, we all have our own taste. Yours might be shaped by what your friends like, what you hear online, and what plays on the local radio station during your commute to school. You probably listen to several genres. Maybe you're even guilty of the cliché "Yeah, I listen to everything except country." But this stage in your life is a great time to broaden your horizons and explore the wonderful variety of music the world has to offer. Beyond "new release" playlists and songs that the algorithm suggests, dive into an unfamiliar genre or search up some classics.

How to Do It

In with the old! New musical genres evolve out of older styles, so try tracing the roots of your favorites. For instance, if you're a hip-hop fanatic, seek out the songs Kendrick Lamar is sampling from—maybe some classic jazz and R & B hits. Chances are you'll find rhythms and styles that draw you in. Or raid a parent's or grandparent's music collection and see where it leads you.

Consult an expert. Do you have a friend with an encyclopedic knowledge of the history of outlaw country or who can recite to you the waves of emo? Ask them to share their favorite playlists or make you a custom playlist as an introduction to the genre.

Go analog. Find a physical record store and browse around. Even if you don't have a record player, you can look for unfamiliar albums that seem interesting and then listen to them via a music streamer. The employees might also have recs!

CAN'T-MISS CLASSICS

Check out these landmark albums to get a sense of some legendary artists' signature styles:

- *Kind of Blue*—ultracool jazz masterpiece by Miles Davis
- *Cello Suites*—Bach's classically perfect six solo works
- *Revolver*—perfect pop/rock songs in every conceivable style by the Beatles
- *12 Greatest Hits*—torch and twang treasures from country queen Patsy Cline
- *The Girl from Ipanema*—Brazilian singer Astrud Gilberto's smooth samba treat
- *To Pimp a Butterfly*—Kendrick Lamar's hip-hop opus

6 Take a Break from Tech

Studies show that American teenagers spend an average of seven to nine hours a day looking at screens. Yes, some of those hours are spent completing schoolwork or other necessary daily tasks, but if we're being honest TikTok, YouTube, and video games take up a lot more of our free time than we'd like to admit. This isn't always bad! As with all things, moderation is key. Spending hours every day scrolling through the endless stream of content in your pocket can leave you feeling drained, apathetic, and lethargic. Escape the algorithm and rest your fried dopamine receptors by putting the screens down, just for a weekend.

How to Do It

Put away devices. Finish up your bingeing, scrolling, and gaming Friday evening in preparation for two full days of tech-free bliss. Sparse phone use is okay if absolutely necessary, but try not to succumb to the enticing pull of social media. If you can't fight the urge by yourself, most phones allow you to set restrictions on certain apps that will lock you out of using them without a certain passcode. Have a family member or friend set the passcode on Friday with the promise that they won't reveal it to you until you've completed your challenge.

Keep busy. What to do with all this newfound free time? Spend the weekend reading a new book, writing in your journal, and taking walks around the neighborhood. Break out the watercolors or finally get around to practicing your clarinet. And don't forget to enjoy some in-person quality time with friends or relatives. It's incredible how much longer the days seem when you're not spending hours scrolling through TikTok. On Monday morning you'll feel refreshed, with a newfound appreciation for time spent in the real world.

TECH-FREE SCHEDULING

Be sure to plan your no-tech weekend for a time when your schedule is actually clear. Living without a cell phone while shuttling from basketball practice to work to a party just isn't going to happen. And your English teacher probably won't take "I was having a no-tech weekend" as an excuse for turning in a handwritten paper.

7 Look Closely at a Work of Art

School field trips to museums can make looking at art seem like work. It's hard to enjoy following a predetermined path through a gallery with an overly enthusiastic tour guide, while tasked with filling out a mandatory worksheet. It's hard to appreciate art in a setting like this. If you're seeking meaningful connection with a work of art, go to a local museum or gallery alone or with a close friend or family member—someone who can appreciate the experience with you and share thoughts and feelings about the works on display.

How to Do It

Choose a starting point. A lot of museums have student or youth discounts. Some offer free admission on certain days of the year. Pick a place you can get to fairly easily and check out its website before you visit. You might end up at a small gallery where you can cover every square foot in an hour. Or you might have access to a huge building with more exhibits than you'll ever have time to see. You might be able to narrow down your starting point to a type of art that seems especially cool to you. If you're not that enthused about paintings, try seeking out jewelry or pottery or textile arts.

Browse. You might choose a temporary exhibit that looks interesting and start there. Or you can randomly roam around until you find a painting, sculpture, photograph, or installation that draws you in. What emotions does it conjure? Does it stir up any memories?

Zoom in. Focus on various aspects of the work, including the artist's use of color, shape, lighting, and symbolism. Consider what the artist might've been trying to show or comment on. Check around the piece for an informational plaque if you want additional expert insight. Or simply let the art speak for itself. If you find yourself drawn to multiple works by the same artist, do some research on that person's life. Understanding an artist's personal experiences can unlock further understanding of their work. Viewing art on a regular basis encourages you to look at the world differently, opening you up to new ideas.

TAKE IT WITH YOU

If a piece really speaks to you, snap a picture of it with your phone (no flash, please). A tiny digital image doesn't really compare to the real thing, but being able to carry favorite art in your pocket is a powerful, creatively inspiring tool. You can also look for a reconstruction or postcard featuring your favorite piece in the museum gift shop. If you build up a sizable collection of artwork photos, consider creating a small photo album or a mosaic of printouts on your bedroom wall.

8 Attend a Theater Performance

If you think theater is dry or stuffy, think again. Theater is an arena for expression, and that means pretty much anything goes. Even in Shakespeare's day, there was scandal and intrigue ruled the stage, with power-hungry characters going all homicidal, relationship drama abounding, and empires being lost. (The plot of *The Winter's Tale* could put *Real Housewives* to shame.) This legacy continues. In the gritty 1990s musical *Rent*, bohemian artists struggle to make ends meet and sustain their dreams. *Hamilton* broke all kinds of Broadway records when it debuted in 2015 with a hip-hop infused retelling of American history. Attending a professional performance of an epic drama (such as *Hamlet* or *The Crucible*) or an edgy musical (such as *Cabaret* or *Chicago*) can be a revelatory experience. You'll laugh, you'll cry . . . you'll find out why your friends knew all the words to the *Wicked* soundtrack even before the movies came out.

How to Do It

Find a show. Check the website of your nearest theater for show listings. You could look for a well-known production or a musical that sounds interesting—maybe a play you've read in school but haven't had a chance to see performed live. If you happen to live in New York, Broadway is in your backyard, and discounted tickets for students are available for shows. If not, performances often tour throughout the country before or after their New York City runs, so you might be able to catch the next *Book of Mormon* in or near your hometown.

Know your budget. For more affordable options, check out local regional theaters or community theaters. Great performances can be found even in very small productions, and when it comes to sets, costumes, and props, a theater can make up for a limited budget with creativity.

FRONT ROW, CENTER AISLE

If you've got a gap in your schedule, you could volunteer to be a theater usher. All you have to do is direct patrons to their seats and point out drinking fountains and bathrooms in the lobby. In exchange, you'll get to see the play for free—and maybe even meet the actors and behind-the-scenes crew at a post-performance party. Contact the theater's administrative offices to sign up.

9 Attend a Local Concert

Do you love live music but don't want to shell out your hard-earned cash for an extortionately priced concert ticket? After service fees, delivery fees, "convenience" fees, and whatever else the sales site likes to throw on top of an already expensive ticket, it can feel like you need to sell a kidney to enjoy live music regularly. And that's assuming bots and scalpers don't scoop up all the tickets seconds after they go on sale.

Fortunately, this isn't the only way. There are probably dozens, if not hundreds, of local artists performing DIY concerts near you for the same price as a meal from McDonald's. Whatever your genre of choice, a bustling scene of talented artists is waiting to be discovered.

How to Do It

Use social media. Search [your city] and [your favorite genre] and scroll until you find a promising-looking artists page or profile. Odds are they'll have a recent post advertising an upcoming show. Check digital flyers for location, ticket price, and names of the artists who'll be performing.

Branch out. Maybe you're already a fan of a local artist. If they have an upcoming performance, go early enough to catch the openers. If you hear something you like, find *that* artist on social media and keep an eye out for their next gig. Rinse and repeat a few times, and before you know it, you'll be a part of your local music scene!

Find the fests. Musicians often perform at local festivals—and not just music-themed festivals. Keep an eye on your county or state fair and on seasonal or cultural celebrations in your area. You might discover a new or under-the-radar talent in between carnival games.

GETTING IN THE GROOVE

You don't need to be a musician to participate in the scene. Without a corporation's deep pockets to help these artists succeed, they rely on community support. If art is your thing, musicians are always looking for people to design flyers and merch. You can work the door, taking ticket payments and making sure the venue doesn't get overcrowded. Or you can volunteer to cover the merch table before, during, or after a show, selling albums and accessories on the artists' behalf.

10 Connect with a Role Model

The best adults in your life try to teach you right from wrong and want to lead you down the right path. You may disagree with them sometimes (and sometimes you may be right), but they have your best interest at heart and can provide much-needed guidance. As they undoubtedly often remind you, they were your age too once, and they probably went through many of the same things you're going through now. It's important to have a role model whose values and actions inspire you.

How to Do It

Look around. You probably already have a role model, even if you don't realize it. It could be a coach, a teacher, or an older cousin. Maybe you love the guitar, and your dad's old high school buddy is a professional musician.

Connect. Simply ask for a bit of this person's time. This can involve an "informational interview" with someone you don't know very well or whose professional path is of special interest to you. Or you can find a less formal and more frequent way to check in. For instance, if you look up to your ballet instructor, offer to help set up before or clean up after class. Don't expect someone to hand you a huge professional opportunity, but feel free to ask how they've gotten to where they are. A good mentor will be happy to share tips about how to get started on the path to achieving your own dreams.

Give back. Role models don't have to be tied to your career path. If you want to learn how to help your community, seek out someone who's done grassroots work in the neighborhood. If you're religious, ask your pastor, rabbi, imam, or other leader what you can do to help those in need. Check out local groups that focus on an issue you care about, and get to know the people who've been involved for a long time. What you learn from them will stay with you long after high school.

FLAWS AND ALL

Throughout your life, your role models will change as you do. You'll outgrow one, connect with another, and one day become a role model for a member of a younger generation. Remember that at the end of the day, role models are just fellow human beings. Don't create an idealized version of your role model in your head. Everyone makes mistakes and has flaws. Emulate your role model's best qualities, feel free to disagree with them on matters you've informed yourself about, and don't hold them to an impossible standard. That said, if a role model turns out to not share a core value with you—one that was key to your respect for and trust of them—it's okay to move on. This is one reason why it's great to have more than one role model, as well as peers who share your values and goals.

11 Develop the Art of Conversation

"Hey, man, what's good?"

"Oh, you know, nothin'. What's good with you?"

"Chillin'."

"Okay, bet."

"Yeah, all right. See ya."

If this sounds like one of your recent conversations, it might be time to raise the bar on your verbal ping-pong. Sure, casual check-ins are like this in some situations, but humans are social animals. We crave meaningful contact with others, and people measure us by what we say and how we say it. Being able to express yourself through the art of conversation is a key life skill. Like any skill, it takes practice.

How to Do It

Break the ice. Next time you're stuck in a communication dead zone, try asking questions: What did you do last weekend? What college are you thinking about going to? Which basketball team are you rooting for in tomorrow's big game? Ask follow-up questions too: What was your favorite song at the concert? How did you decide on that college as your top choice? When did you become a Knicks fan?

Look engaged. Put your conversational partner at ease by maintaining frequent (but not necessarily constant) eye contact, smiling, and doing your best to not cut them off mid-sentence. Make sure they know you're listening and are interested in what they have to say.

Find common ground. It's fun to bond over shared concerns and complaints: too much homework, dating woes, the Chiefs are in the Super Bowl *again*. Once you've got a starting point, you'll find it easier to connect.

READ THE ROOM

Pick the right moments to engage in deep conversation with someone. The cashier at the grocery store probably doesn't want to be locked into a fifteen-minute discussion about your day while a line of impatient customers grows behind you. But no matter how short the exchange, always be cordial and polite. It can make someone's day just to see a friendly smile, and even a brief surface-level interaction can have a positive impact on you too.

12 Make a Public Speech

Do you suffer from glossophobia? That's the fear of public speaking, one of the most common phobias in the world. Even the most outgoing person can get a bit nervous in front of a crowd—whether that crowd is made up of classmates, bosses, or complete strangers. The pressure to wow them with your expertise, or even just hold their attention, can be overwhelming. But with a few helpful tricks and plenty of practice, you can hone your public speaking skills, even if you're still nervous on the inside.

How to Do It

Write your speech. Put all your thoughts into a messy first draft. Then organize your ideas. Do any background research that's needed. Imagine what questions your audience might ask and provide answers.

Keep it short and sweet. Start by giving your audience a reason to care about your topic. Then dive in. Use simple, conversational, precise language; don't worry about trying to sound sophisticated. Just say what you mean as clearly as you can. Wrap up by briefly restating your main points.

Know your audience. In a class presentation, you can reference material you've already covered or stuff you learned in last year's shared curriculum. If you're talking to peers you're usually comfortable with, feel free to throw in some jokes. If you're talking to adults in a formal setting, minimize the slang.

Practice! Read your speech out loud several times. You don't have to have it completely memorized, but get familiar with how it sounds. Even if you plan to read from your script, you'll be less likely to stumble if you know it pretty well. This is also a good way to check that the speech isn't too long—or too short—for your allotted time. Read the speech to yourself in the mirror, keeping a close eye on your facial expressions and vocal inflections. Speak as naturally as possible; *feel* the words as you say them.

Keep calm. If you're able to hold a small item like a coin or a pebble, this can help steady you. Speak more slowly than you think you need to; it's easy to rush. Look up from your paper or your phone occasionally, even if it's only at the beginning or the end of your speech. If looking directly at your audience makes you nervous, focus on a spot slightly over their heads. If you're shaky from nerves or if your voice sounds weird, remember that your audience probably can't tell. Trust that people are focusing on your words—and that if they were in your place, they'd be just as nervous as you are, if not more so!

LEARN FROM THE MASTERS

Study how your favorite comedian captivates their audience. They might begin with a statement, tell a story to back up their stance, then revisit the original statement, which becomes the punch line. Great speeches have similar patterns. Make a statement, back it up with evidence, then revisit your original point.

13 Interpret a Dream

Did you know your dreams can have deep meanings? Many psychologists believe dreams are your mind's way of expressing unconscious thoughts, feelings, urges, memories that you're not otherwise aware of. Analyzing these dreams, even casually, can give you deeper insight into your psyche.

How to Do It

Start a journal. Keep a dream journal on your nightstand or make a dedicated document in your phone's notes app. As soon as you wake up, write down as many details from your dreams as you can remember.

Ponder the pieces. Read over your notes and think about what each aspect of the dream might symbolize. If you're stuck, the internet is full of interpretations of common or general dream elements. If your dreams aren't too embarrassing, share them with a close friend and swap interpretations.

Keep it light. Remember not to take any of this too seriously. Dream interpretation should be treated as a fun thought exercise, not a serious psychological assessment.

BAD DREAMS

Having an occasional scary dream is normal, but if you're having a lot of nightmares, you should talk to someone about it. You may need to simply adjust some parts of your pre-sleep routine—like when you put away your screens for the night or how dark your bedroom is—to get a more peaceful rest. Or you might need support in dealing with real-life anxieties that are seeping into your dreams. A trusted adult can help you figure out a solution.

POPULAR DREAMS

Many dreams are unique to the person who has them. But there are also lots of common themes that people share in their dreams. Here are some examples:

- falling from a high place
- being chased
- teeth falling out
- being late for an important deadline, like a test
- spiders, snakes, and other creatures

14 Connect with an Animal

Are you a dog lover without enough space to keep a four-legged friend in your home? Do you love cats . . . until you start sneezing uncontrollably after two or three hours of dander exposure? Maybe you have a thing for horses but have never actually ridden one?

Humans and animals can form special bonds based on mutual respect and a yearning for companionship. Studies show that being around animals can lower your levels of cortisol, a stress-related hormone and improve your mood. Even if a pet isn't in the cards, you can still find ways to spend some time with animals.

How to Do It

Volunteer. Your local humane society could likely use all the extra hands it can get. You can help by walking dogs, feeding and grooming pets, or even updating the shelter's website in between giving belly rubs. Offering a scared, lonely animal some much-needed one-on-one attention is its own reward—but it also looks good on college apps.

Spend some cash. If you're a horse person, search for a stable that offers professional horseback riding lessons or trail rides for beginners. To meet a different kind of furry friend, visit a farm that raises alpacas or sheep. Or keep an eye out for a "goat yoga" session in your area.

Admire from afar. You don't have to get up close to an animal to appreciate it. Spend an afternoon birdwatching. Go for a walk at rabbit o'clock (early evening). Or watch the dramas unfolding among the squirrels in a backyard. Don't feed undomesticated animals, but take as many photos as you like.

DON'T HORSE AROUND

Treat animals with care and gentleness. Respect their space—especially if you cross paths with a wild animal. (You don't want to join the ranks of people who've been gored by a bison after getting too close.) Around domesticated creatures, follow caretakers' instructions for how to hold, pet, or approach them.

15 Join a Club

Do you have interests that you're dying to talk about but that earn only eye-rolls from your friends? Well, it's not your fault they have no taste. No matter how "weird" or obscure your hobby or obsession—from A24 films to Warhammer figure painting to Japanese fashion—fellow fanatics are out there. Online communities are an obvious way to connect with kindred spirits, but you can also sign up for an in-person club. You may only have one thing in common with the other members, but for one night each month, you'll have a blast geeking out over your shared love.

How to Do It

Find your people. Search online for local meetups of hobby enthusiasts. Many groups use social media to plan events and attract new members, but a simple browser search should also give you some leads. If you can't find a local group that gathers regularly, keep an eye out for a convention that's close enough to attend. Cons happen all over the country throughout the year. Some are for specific fandoms; some are for a big umbrella of interests. If you're passionate about a band or a solo musical artist, they might have a periodic fan club meetup near you. Join a local book club to discuss your latest fantasy epic obsession.

Multitask. If you want to learn a new skill while you socialize, check out your nearest community center or a social media page for local clubs. You may find options for all sorts of activities: conversational Spanish, advanced chess, poetry writing, and tae kwon do.

Do it yourself. If you can't find a local club in your area of interest, gauge interest for starting one yourself by posting on social media, or ask a friend with a shared interest if they already have a network of like-minded people. Always be vigilant for creepy behavior when socializing with strangers. It's a good idea to attend meetups with a trusted adult or with friends, at least until you get the lay of the land.

DIGITAL FAN CLUB

Social media makes it easy to connect with people who share your interests. You can easily find a Discord server or a subreddit filled with discussions about your favorite thing. Use good digital security practices, though. Choose a forum with robust moderation policies so that inappropriate behavior is less likely—and easier to deal with if it pops up. Don't divulge personal information like where you live or your full name. Keep discussions focused on the main topic.

16 Host a Film Festival

Film festivals are held all over the world as glamorous showcases for Hollywood blockbusters and independent films. These fests aren't limited to entertainment capitals like LA, New York, and Berlin—they happen regularly in towns across the country. If you're a film aficionado but can't yet attend Cannes or Sundance, you can start your own festival from the comfort of your home. With carefully selected programs, a cozy screening space, and exclusive invitations to a few lucky friends, you can put those high-minded snobfests to shame.

How to Do It

Explore options. Browse whatever streaming services you can access to see what's available. Your local library may also have movies you can check out, either digitally or as physical media. Cataloging and reviewing sites like Letterboxd can help you find films that've slipped under the box office's radar. Skip the most popular titles in favor of little-known gems that will expand the cinematic horizons of your attendees. Picking a theme can help you narrow down your options. You can do a night of animated classics, musicals, or films about animals.

STREAMING SCHEME

If a film you're dying to see is only available on a streaming service you don't subscribe to, you can set up a subscription (maybe it offers a temporary free trial) and cancel it as soon as your festival concludes.

Finalize your lineup. If your fest will take place over a single day, three films should be plenty. You might pick movies you love and want to share with friends—or movies that are totally new to you. If you're able to stretch it out over an entire weekend, choose five or six films, but don't feel pressured to watch them all if you feel yourselves getting burned out.

Make it fancy. Provide beverages and snacks—or arrange for each friend to contribute a refreshment. Encourage attendees to dress up; you can imitate a glamorous Hollywood look or wear something that fits with the fest's theme. Have everyone set their phones aside during the viewing so that the films can get your full attention.

MAKING A MINI FEST

Want to host a film fest but don't have six hours? Pull together a mini fest with a handful of friends. Together, choose a super-specific theme—like favorite kitschy musical number or most iconic love story. Have each person pick a favorite scene from a movie based on that theme. Then have everyone prepare their clips (lots of movie clips are easy to find on YouTube) and play the scenes back-to-back at the mini fest. This way you can see parts of various movies and learn a little about each of your friends.

17 Throw a House Party

Parties can raise a ton of questions: Who's hosting? How many people are going to show up? Will the parents be home? Is Spencer going to puke on my shoes? When you're the host, it's important to plan carefully so your get-together doesn't go off the rails. Your goals—for yourself and your attendees—are to have fun, be safe, and avoid property damage.

How to Do It

Clear it with adults. If a parent says no, don't go behind their back. You don't want to risk a months-long grounding for one night of fun. Instead, ask what would make them comfortable with you hosting a party. How might you show that you can be trusted? What ground rules would put them at ease? They might be more flexible than you expect. Some parents are okay with a party at their house if they're home, or if everyone leaves by a specific time.

Send invites. Limit your guest list to close friends and a few people you'd like to get to know better. Be clear about the ground rules: When does the party end? What substances are absolutely not welcome on the premises?

Make your space party-ready. No need to go all-out with refreshments, but provide some snacks and beverages. Carefully craft a playlist to match the vibe you're going for—whether you want to kick the party up a notch or keep things mellow and conversation-friendly.

PARTY SMARTER, NOT HARDER

To prevent your first house party from being your last, follow these guidelines:

1. Tell any immediate neighbors about your plans in advance. Tell them to call *you*, not the cops, if things get too loud.
2. Remove all breakables, such as vases and picture frames, from the space. Even the most well-behaved guest might bump into something while dancing.
3. Be vigilant about alcohol and other substances. You don't want anyone getting hurt, sick, or into legal trouble. Even if your house is substance free, be aware if somebody has pregamed, and don't let anyone drive home after drinking. Underage drinking and driving has serious legal consequences and puts everyone on the road in danger.
4. Make sure the guest list doesn't get out of control. Word of a party can spread like wildfire through social media. If too many people show up, shut the party down.
5. Keep trash cans, paper towels, and disinfectant on hand.
6. Tidy up when the party's over.

18 Read One Another's Palms

Life is so unpredictable. It's impossible to know what will happen tomorrow, let alone one, ten, or fifty years from now. Our future is shaped by a combination of luck and our own choices. But it can be fun to experiment with fortune-telling practices like numerology, tarot cards, and the Magic 8 Ball.

While most people have little faith in the pseudoscience of chiromancy—or palm reading—there's no harm in dabbling. It can be a tool for self-reflection . . . or at least make for an entertaining afternoon.

How to Do It

Assemble your readers. Gather with a few friends with open minds and open palms. Take turns studying the three most prominent lines on one another's palms.

Know your lines. The heart line is near the top of the palm. Its length and depth are thought to represent your love life, emotional stability, and blood-pumping health. The head line, which starts at the edge of the palm under the index finger, supposedly indicates your intellectual and creative abilities.

The life line runs from the edge of your palm above the thumb and forms an arc as it reaches your wrist. Believers will tell you that this line represents physical health and overall vitality and energy. Other lines that crisscross the three biggies include the sun line, fate line, and Girdle of Venus.

Interpret freely. To get diagrams for reference, check out online illustrations. Without taking it too seriously, see what the fates may (or may not) have in store for you.

SHAKE ON IT

Once your palm-reading session has ended, keep your hands working by inventing a secret handshake for your circle of friends. Whether it's a high-five adaptation or a spin-off of signals used in baseball practice, a secret handshake mystifies outsiders and ties friends together.

19 End an Argument

With all that's going on in your life, the last thing you need is extra drama. But conflict happens even in the healthiest, most supportive friendships. You can't avoid it entirely; you *can* deal with it in a mature way.

Let's focus on a petty argument: A small annoyance or miscommunication spirals into a larger problem. It can be easy to mistake a well-intentioned comment ("You've gotta work on your field goals if you wanna make varsity," or "Are you sure about those pants?") for a vicious put-down. Or you might finally lose patience with a habit that's been annoying you for ages and say something harsh.

Some relationships *will* come and go, but strong friendships will weather storms. Whether you're the offended party or the culprit, or a little of both, it's worthwhile to try to patch things up.

How to Do It

Think it through. Give yourself a chance to calm down. During an argument, your brain releases stress hormones like epinephrine and cortisol, which can make it difficult to think clearly. Take a few deep breaths. Acknowledge how you're feeling. Then consider what actually happened: Who's upset with whom, and why? What exactly was said, done, or not done? Did the other person act out of character, or is this a recurring issue? Do you need to take accountability for any of your behavior, whether you "started it" or not?

Apologize. If you're the one to blame, own up to your mistake. You might be tempted to hope it'll just blow over, but taking responsibility is important. Make it clear that you understand *what* you did wrong and will try to do better in the future. If your apology isn't accepted right away, don't keep pushing. Give your friend space. If you're close, chances are they'll ultimately be able to forgive you.

Be clear. If you've been hurt by someone else's actions, make sure they *know* you're upset. Maybe your friend blew off plans or insulted your taste in music. It might be obvious to *you* that this was hurtful, but they may not have even registered it. Reach out in a non-accusatory way: "Hey, I don't think you meant to hurt my feelings, but what you said about Led Zeppelin really bummed me out." They may apologize and promise to do better. Or they may get defensive. They may even reveal a deeper issue that you need to work through.

THE TEXTING TRAP

Try not to get drawn into a long text conversation, which can escalate arguments instead of resolving them. See if the other person is willing to talk face-to-face. It's easier to communicate when you can see facial expressions and hear tone.

Move forward. A trustworthy friend will apologize for hurtful behavior and commit to not making it a pattern. But what if you're *both* certain the other person's in the wrong? For a minor squabble, it can be enough to agree that nobody intended to be hurtful and to let bygones be bygones.

20 Make a Friend in Another Country

For most of human history, people have made friends with the people who live near them. You might have friends who go to your school or play on a team with you. You might even have online friends who live in another part of the country. But what about a friend who lives halfway around the world?

Corresponding with someone from another country is a great way to learn about different cultures, practice your communication skills, and work on your fluency in a second language (or at least learn some key foreign phrases). Most important, you'll form a bond with a new friend, even if the two of you don't meet face-to-face.

How to Do It

Find a connection. You might already be connected with someone from another country through social media. Maybe you follow your friend's Japanese cousin on Instagram or share a Discord server with a mutual from India. If you've verified that this person is who they say they are and that they're around your age, you might start chatting with them privately. Alternatively, your school might host a pen pal program with other schools around the world, or you can find a pen pal program online.

Send a message. Email or instant messaging is easy, but snail mail can actually be more fun. You can add photos, cute stickers, and other fun memorabilia to your letters. Break the ice by talking about hobbies, books, movies, or favorite foods. Ask the other person about their interests and daily life.

Write on a routine. Make a goal for how often you'll write, depending on how long it takes your communication to reach the recipient. You don't always have to wait for a response before sending another note, but you don't want the correspondence to be totally one-sided. And responding to your pal's latest note gives you more to say!

CAN I BORROW TEN BUCKS?

If your pen pal starts complaining about money problems—or asks you outright for a loan or gift—you might be dealing with a scammer. Stop the correspondence right away if anything seems suspicious.

21 Make a Gift

Exchanging thoughtful gifts with friends and family on birthdays and holidays is a fun tradition and a good way to show your appreciation for your loved ones. If you really want to do something unique, give handmade gifts. Your one-of-a-kind creations will make more of an impression than a coffee-chain gift card. Making your own present will also probably save you some money! And it gives you a chance to explore your creative side.

How to Do It

Use your skills. Are you a whiz in the kitchen? Plan to bake some delicious treats. Can you knit? Get cracking on a scarf.

Gather what you need. You can stock up on craft supplies or shelf-stable ingredients months in advance so you're not spending a bunch of money all at once or rushing to find stuff at the last minute. Do you have an eye for fashion? A trip to the thrift store can yield some cheap accessories waiting to be transformed and personalized. Are you strapped for cash but good at writing? Craft a short story or a poem in honor of the recipient.

Give yourself enough time. If you're taking an art, woodworking, or metalsmithing class on the weekends or as an elective in school, figure out how long it'll take you to make a giftable custom item. If you're crocheting a blanket, calculate when you need to start.

Make it personal. Tailor your gifts to the receivers. Use their favorite colors. With food, account for dietary restrictions and preferences. Ask yourself if your friend will actually want to wear this punked-up belt with all the cool studs and grommets you've added.

Keep it in perspective. When in doubt, remember: it's the thought that counts. Don't go broke or stress yourself out trying to create the perfect present. Even a carefully designed card on fancy stationery can make for a perfect keepsake.

TIME IS OF THE ESSENCE

People tend to buy gifts instead of making them because the latter takes *much* more time. Sure, that TikTok candle-making tutorial looked easy enough, but if you're embarking on a new project, factor in time for mistakes and do-overs.

22 Start a Book Club

Losing yourself in a good book is one of life's most rewarding solitary activities. But sometimes you need to discuss that book with *other people.* Forming a book club is a great way to share your thoughts—and discover new ideas to chew on.

It's also a great way to introduce nonreaders to a love of the written word. If that nonreader is you, the promise of a night of snacks and socializing might be the motivation you need. Book clubs are meant to be *fun*. The point is to escape the rigid confines of your English class and enjoy literature on your terms.

How to Do It

Choose a theme. It can be a specific genre. Or it can be young adult novels of any genre, or books written by authors of a particular background, or even just books that fit a certain page count range. (Starting with short books can be a good way to get people in the habit of reading.)

Invite members. Recruit four to eight friends who can commit to meeting regularly—maybe once a month, depending on people's schedules. Invite people who you think will actually take the time to read the book, not someone who'll consult SparkNotes twenty minutes beforehand.

Come up with a schedule. Choose meeting dates and locations; members can take turns hosting.

Make a book list. The whole club can come up with this list together. You can vote on what you'll read first (and then what you'll read next), or you can let each member take a turn picking a book. Don't rule out something you've read already. It'll be interesting to hear others' interpretations of books you think you know inside and out.

Have a structure. Meetings can be super informal, with wide-ranging discussions. But you'll want to cover certain key elements of each book you read. Talk about plot points, themes, and major characters. Share likes and dislikes. And don't be afraid to admit if there was something you didn't quite get! Chances are you're not alone—and you probably picked up on something that somebody else missed.

GENIUS IN EVERY GENRE

Some adults you know might turn up their noses at "genre" fiction—basically any category of fiction that emphasizes plot at least as much as character development. But there are skilled writers, brilliant storytelling, thought-provoking themes, *and* great characters to be found in any genre. Here are some genres to check out:

- fantasy
- historical fiction
- horror
- mystery
- romance
- science fiction

23 Sing Karaoke

Screaming along to your favorite songs while you're alone in the shower can be fun, but doesn't it feel like it's missing something? Your Coachella-worthy performance deserves to be heard by an audience of more than shampoo bottles and body wash. Even if your vocals aren't quite ready for the festival circuit, gathering a bunch of friends for karaoke can be tons of fun.

How to Do It

Find your scene. Most cities have at least one all-ages karaoke club or bar where teens are welcome to channel their inner pop star. If nothing is available near you, gather your friends in a nonjudgmental home and search for karaoke versions of your favorite songs on YouTube or a music streamer.

Choose your songs. Most karaoke establishments have long lists of songs to choose from. It's a good idea to come with a few ideas and then check for those specific songs. You can always browse the offerings more thoroughly once you've put in a few requests. You'll likely have some downtime while you wait for strangers to perform—unless you rent a private karaoke room. If your karaoke room is the internet, you'll find tons of instrumental tracks with lyrics that run across the screen for when you're laughing too hard to remember the words.

Don't take it too seriously. You're not getting signed by a record label tonight. You're here to have fun. Don't worry if your voice isn't in top form. Choose a song that's fun to sing, and go all out, but don't sweat botched lyrics or sharp notes.

Don't hog the spotlight. Make sure everyone gets ample time to live out their rock star dreams. If you're in public, be a respectful audience while other patrons are onstage. Encourage shy friends to participate by choosing songs that are perfect for group sing-alongs.

WHO INVENTED KARAOKE?

Karaoke means "empty orchestra" in Japanese. The practice was started by Japanese drummer Daisuke Inoue in Kobe in the 1970s. Inoue and his band often played gigs for wealthy business leaders who liked to sing along. One time, a businessman asked the drummer to accompany him on a vacation to play music for him and his singing buddies. Inoue couldn't go, so he made the businessman a cassette tape of his music to take with him. It was such a success that Inoue and his friends started making custom tapes for clients and selling them along with singing machines. Thus, karaoke was born.

24 Dine High-End on a Low Budget

Fast food is cheap, and you don't have to worry about what size fork to use when you're tearing into a burrito bowl at the mall's food court. But sometimes it's good to slow down and enjoy a different dining experience. Fancy restaurants are not off-limits just because the salmon meuniere is out of your price range. If you choose the place carefully and order smartly, you can eat at a restaurant that uses real china and cloth napkins without breaking the bank.

How to Do It

Consult the ratings. Search the internet for reviews of upscale restaurants in or near your town. (Google and Yelp reviews aren't always the most accurate sources, but they're good starting places. Your local paper might occasionally run a "10 Best New Restaurants" article.

Pick a place and a plate. Prioritize the three A's: atmosphere, accessibility, and appetizers. If you don't want to be stuck washing dishes in the back of the restaurant to pay off your bill, keep your eye on the starters section of the menu. Order only one small plate per person, or you'll end up paying just as you would for entrées. Stick with water as your beverage rather than an expensive mocktail. Water tastes much better when it's served in a fancy glass and delicately poured by a tuxedoed server.

Tip generously. Restaurant staff rely on tips for much of their income, and gratuity shows your appreciation for their service. Leave at least 15 percent, even if the service wasn't stellar. If your service was truly excellent, kick that up to 20 or 25 percent, depending on what you can afford.

A SWEET WAY TO SAVE

Another way to have a fine-dining experience while broke: skip dinner altogether and go right for dessert. If the restaurant's generally busy, go a bit later in the evening, after the dinner rush is over. (Restaurants don't want people to take up tables with small orders during dinnertime.) Order hot chocolate and cheesecake, and soak up the ambiance.

25 Take a Road Trip

If you can spare the time and gas money, taking a road trip is a teenage rite of passage and a great way to bond with your friends while exploring a new locale. Even if you only drive a few towns over to enjoy a hike or visit older friends who've gone off to college, you'll experience a newfound sense of freedom and personal responsibility. Don't take this responsibility *too* lightly. Leaving your town means that if you run into any problems on your journey, you're more or less on your own. But if you have the right group of friends, a stocked car, and a semi-set itinerary (leaving some room for spontaneous detours), you'll be ready to set off on your adventure.

How to Do It

Assemble a crew. Include at least two people who have a driver's license so no one's stuck behind the wheel for the entire trip. Your crew should be both responsible and easygoing. You don't want a lunatic driver speeding down the freeway or a high-maintenance passenger who demands you stop for bathroom breaks every few miles.

DON'T FORGET!

Here's a basic packing list for the road:

- full water bottles
- snacks (check in about food allergies ahead of time)
- a real map, in case you find yourself without cell service
- a phone charger
- a change of clothes
- a road trip playlist
- enough money to cover expenses, plus a little extra

Set your itinerary. Agree on where you're headed, when you'll be returning, and where you'll stay in between if the trip is longer than a day. If you're staying somewhere overnight, make sure that it's in a safe environment, like a friend's house, and that it has room for all of you.

Agree on a budget. Don't stick the owner of the car with all the gas expenses, and make sure other expenses are doled out relatively equally. If your friend pays for your lunch, volunteer to cover their gas station-snack purchases.

Put safety first. Check the car before you leave. You don't want to notice a maintenance light *after* driving five hundred miles. Make sure your phones are charged. Confirm that your parents or guardians know exactly where you're headed and how long you'll be gone. Check in at regular intervals on a longer trip; even a brief "made to X" text will save the adults a world of worry.

TEAM EFFORT

Music streaming apps allow you to create collaborative playlists that multiple users can add songs to simultaneously. Create a road trip playlist and add all the passengers to it. That way, if someone has a song they want to hear, they can just add it to the playlist rather than try to wrestle the aux away from the driver.

26 Research Your Family Tree

You might've made a basic family tree for a school project at some point. But have you ever challenged yourself to trace your family's roots as far back as possible? Piecing together the names, birthdates, and origins of your ancestors can reveal a lot about how you came to exist. Subjects you've learned about in school can suddenly become real—not simply textbook filler for you to memorize but actual experiences that your relatives lived through. If you're adopted or otherwise separated from your biological family, you can do this for either your adopted parents or your biological ones. Both investigations will turn up interesting (and possibly very different) results.

How to Do It

Talk to relatives. If possible, ask parents or grandparents what they know about the family's history. What countries did ancestors emigrate from? Who first came to the US and when? Has the family name been "Americanized"?

Make a chart. Create a hand-drawn genealogy chart or find a customizable family tree tool online. Genealogy websites allow you to access historical documents like census records, marriage certificates, and newspaper articles.

These can be helpful for tracing your family tree, especially if your family has been in the US for a while. Fill in blanks as you discover the names and origins of various relatives.

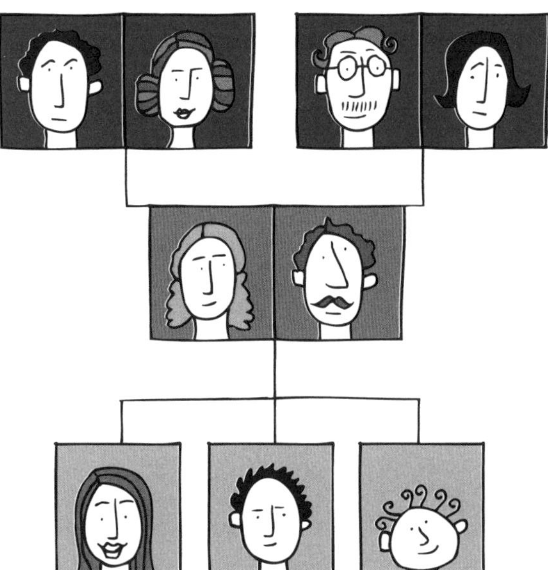

Accept unknowns. Not every family has the benefit of a clear paper trail. You may never find out who your

DNA DILEMMA

Biotech companies allow people over eighteen to send in DNA samples for analysis. The tests they perform on these samples can uncover your unique genetic profile, granting you insights into your family's ethnic and geographic history. They can even connect you with long-lost relatives who've also used the service. But if sending your DNA in a vial to a corporation seems a little Big Brothery to you, stick with other methods of investigation.

great-grandma's real dad was or when your distant ancestors arrived on the continent. Make peace with the fact that you'll never know everything about your family history.

Preserve for posterity. Keep all information you find. Back up any digital records in case the site you're using isn't around forever. Future generations will thank you for doing the research and might be able to build off it with new tools.

DIGGING FOR BURIED ROOTS

Descendants of enslaved Black people may not know their ancestors' names, birthdates, or countries of origin due to limited record-keeping by enslavers. But an investigator still has options. Surnames can be clues about not just direct ancestors but about ancestors' enslavers; people are sometimes able to trace parts of their genealogy through plantations those enslavers owned and communities nearby. Some survivors of slavery ran ads in newspapers seeking lost loved ones. Many of these ads have been preserved and even digitized, offering details that can help people identify ancestors. And new tools and records turn up all the time.

27 Reach Out to a Long-Lost Relative

While it's fun to piece together family history, there's plenty of investigating to do with family members who are still alive. Somewhere out there you have relatives you've never met and probably never even knew existed! (If you're adopted and doing this with your unknown biological family, you may be in for an even more challenging and fascinating journey.) By reaching out to a long-lost relative, you'll make genetic, geographical, and emotional connections.

How to Do It

Talk to close relatives. See if they know about any distant relations floating around out there. It could be someone they know but lost touch with, or it could be somebody they've only heard about.

Check online. Pursue an online family tree project until you've turned up names and contact info that your parents and grandparents never had. If someone in your family uses Facebook, the friend recommendation algorithm has probably (unsettlingly) already turned up some distant relatives.

Follow the trail. You might hit some dead ends—old addresses or phone numbers, or someone who's passed on. But you may find a long-lost family member who'll be thrilled to connect. If they live too far away for an in-person meeting, set up a phone call or a video chat.

Have a conversation. Come up with a few questions for your relative in advance so you don't have to worry about running out of things to say. This isn't an interview, so you don't have to stick to those topics. You can also tell this new relative about yourself. They'll probably have a few questions for you too! Don't get super personal right away, but feel free to share hobbies, favorite foods, and family lore.

SAFETY FIRST

Stay vigilant when talking to any adult you don't know. Be alert for any signs of creepiness, and never agree to meet up with someone by yourself, even if they claim to be your aunt's-cousin's-uncle.

28 Record an Oral History

Uncle Joe is always good for an after-dinner walk down memory lane. Why not get some of those tales on record? Lots of people in your life probably have interesting stories about their childhoods, wild college days, failed business ventures, and other unique experiences. But these stories can be lost or distorted by time. The best way to preserve family stories is to record them as told by the people who lived them. By acting as the family story collector, you can learn a lot about history—from wars to economic depressions to pop culture, art, and dating rituals—and how it affected your family.

How to Do It

Arrange an interview. Ask a cool, older relative if you can do an oral history project with them. Though hitting the Record button while Uncle Joe is mid-rant may be tempting, it's best to give the interviewee advance warning. That gives them ample time to iron out the details of the story in their head and decide what they'd like to share for posterity.

Set up a time and place. You'll want to be somewhere quiet enough to record. Allot about two hours for each session. Any less and you won't have time to dive into details. Any more and you run the risk of wearing out your subject. You can always schedule additional sessions if you couldn't get to everything in a single day.

Choose a recording method. Depending on what your subject is comfortable with, you can record just audio or take a video of your interview. You can use your phone or bring a laptop and portable microphone if you're going for higher production quality. Test your method in advance. It's not a bad idea to have a backup method

Bring a list of questions. You'll probably veer quite a bit from the list as you go along, but it's helpful to have some ideas jotted down in case the conversation stalls. Make sure your subject knows they can stop recording at any time if they feel uncomfortable, and that you can edit out a section if they accidentally let slip something they shouldn't say on record.

Save your work. When you're done, save the original recording. Back it up to a cloud server as well. If you make any edits, save the new version separately. There's nothing worse than losing hours of work to a corrupted file!

WHAT TO ASK

Start with biographical details: date and place of birth, family names, marriage history. But encourage your subject to go on tangents as other memories will come up. Make sure you get details—that's the juicy stuff. "So you said you were born *seven* months after your parents were married?" "Uncle Joe brought *how* many girlfriends home?" Preface delicate follow-up questions with "Can I ask if . . ." or "Would you be willing to say more about . . ."

29 Spend Quality Time with Grandparents

Some people have involved grandparents who play an active and important role in their lives. For others, Grandma and Grandpa are kindly but somewhat distant folks who show up once or twice a year. Assuming they're safe and supportive people to be around, it's a good idea to spend quality time with them while you have the chance. Right now, it may seem like a drag to spend a day away from your friends, but when your grandparents are no longer around, you'll cherish every moment you spent with them. If they've already passed on, keep their memories close by looking at photos, listening to oral histories, flipping through scrapbooks, and talking to other relatives about them.

How to Do It

Set a routine. If any of your grandparents live nearby, set aside at least one afternoon or evening each month to spend with them. If you have any siblings that want to tag along, all the better. But if not, one-on-one time can be even more valuable. For grandparents who live far away, a regular video chat is a great way to keep in touch.

Plan activities. Take their health, mobility, and interests into account. If they're active, you can go on an outing. Or the plan can be simple: dinner and a movie at home, listening to old records from their youth, snacks and conversation.

Share stories. When hanging out at home, invite them to show you photo albums, baby books, and other keepsakes. Tell them about your life too—your grades, your friends, what you're planning to do after high school. Ask them about their lives when they were your age. In some ways, your life is completely, fascinatingly different from your grandparents' younger days. But you may also find some aspects surprisingly similar.

ANCIENT WISDOM

Your grandparents have probably acquired some secret talents over their long lives. Encourage them to show off their skills. If your grandpa spent decades as a chef, ask him for some recipes. Is your grandma an avid gardener? See if she'll gift you some plant cuttings or guide you through a trip to the garden center.

30 Make Peace with a Sibling

Siblings can be mostly okay, but when you spend your whole life living under the same roof as somebody, conflict is certain to arise from time to time. It can be big or small, inconsequential or catastrophic, lighthearted or cold-blooded. Moving past it is a skill. Maybe your parents have helped mediate in the past, but as you become adults, you'll want to resolve these flare-ups yourselves. Next time you find yourself in a nasty altercation with a sibling, do your best to be the peacemaker—even if you're sure you're right. And if you can't fully clear the air, try not to hold on to a grudge.

How to Do It

Hold up. When a situation gets heated, pause, take a deep breath, and *don't* say the first thing that occurs to you.

Find the humor. The problem you're fighting over might seem pretty ridiculous once you take a step back and think about it. When in doubt, shift the emphasis away from your differences to what you have in common—for instance, how much your parents drive you nuts. It'll help you remember you two are actually on the same team.

Create some space. Take time apart to cool down, especially if you're arguing about something serious. Maybe spend some time at a friend's house and get their third-party opinion on the situation. By the time you cross paths with your sibling again, you might both be over what happened. And if not, you'll be able to talk through the situation more calmly.

Talk through the big stuff. If you're dealing with a serious or recurring source of tension, it's better to address it head on than to let it fester. Tell your sibling that you've thought about the situation and are seeking a resolution, not just to reopen old wounds. Try not to accuse them of anything; instead, focus on what would help you peacefully coexist again—for a little while longer anyway.

COMMUNICATION STATION

Here are some tips for having a tricky conversation with a sibling (or anyone):

- Explain where you're coming from—how you're feeling, what your goal is.
- Apologize for anything you said or did that was out of line or that they may have found hurtful.
- Say "I would find it really helpful if . . ." or "I would really appreciate . . ." instead of "You need to . . ."

31 Plan a Family Outing

Oh, the dreaded family outing. Whether it's yet another staging of the *Nutcracker*, a painfully boring family reunion, or a catastrophic camping weekend, you may find yourself counting down the hours until you can get some quality time *alone*. Maybe your family takes "quality time" to the extreme. Maybe familial tensions are exacerbated in a new environment that brings its own stresses. But if everyone involved is well-intentioned, it's possible to pull off an outing that doesn't descend into chaos or boredom and might even be . . . fun.

How to Do It

Make a proposal. Tell your parents that if they provide the cash (as needed), you'll do all the heavy lifting to plan a fun outing.

Decide where to go. Choose an activity that everyone can participate in. If you're all relatively active, you might pick apples at an orchard, zoom around town on electric scooters, or snow tube down an icy hill. If your family isn't outdoorsy, find an interesting museum exhibition, book an escape room, or go bowling.

Handle logistics. Figure out the cost and travel time. Check the forecast to plan an outdoor activity, and have a rain-check option. If the budget's tight, look for a free activity like visiting a nature preserve, browsing a local art fair, attending a movie in the park.

Have an *inning*. If weather, finances, or transportation are an issue, organize a joint activity at home. See how much progress you can make on a one-thousand-piece puzzle while listening to a narrative podcast or some music you can all agree on. Or if you enjoy a healthy competition, set up a board game night. This way, you can channel your desire to destroy your sibling in a way that won't require medical intervention.

ONE-ON-ONES

Spending time with the whole family is great, but it's equally vital that you get one-on-one time with each parent or guardian. Be sure to spend quality time with just Mom or Dad every once in a while, even if it's just an ice-cream run or a walk around the block. No siblings, aunts, or grandparents to distract you, just good old-fashioned parental bonding.

32 Cook a Meal from Scratch

"What's for dinner?" If you're usually the one asking this question, try answering it one night (undoubtedly to the shock and delight of your household's resident chef). Cooking a three-course dinner might seem daunting if your previous preparations have been limited to late-night pizza rolls, but the process can be exciting and empowering. Cooking is a valuable life skill that will pay dividends for you down the road (not to mention impress future dates). So grab an apron and fire extinguisher, and get cooking!

How to Do It

Learn the basics. If your family has a physical cookbook, flip through it. Search the internet for recipe blogs or social media accounts related to cooking. You can find tons of videos that break down recipes step-by-step for a general audience.

Choose your recipes. Start with something simple yet tasty. As your skills grow, you can gradually expand your comfort zone and get more adventurous. Be mindful of the preferences and dietary restrictions of the people you're cooking for. You don't want to unveil a roast duck to a bunch of vegetarians.

WEEKNIGHT WONDERS

There's no shame in making a quick, easy meal—especially when time is limited! Here are some flexible staples:

- **Pasta with pizzazz.** Sauté or roast some seasoned vegetables to mix in with your cooked and drained pasta, or throw some greens into the warm pasta and water before draining. Add some olive oil if you don't have or want a sauce.
- **Rice and beans for the win.** With tomatoes, onion, garlic, and some spices, you can get several hearty meals out of a big batch. Add lentils for extra protein.
- **Grilled anything sandwich.** Give the cheese (or vegan equivalent) some company with some apple slices, grilled or roasted red peppers, tomatoes, or meat. (But probably not all at once.)

Deal with details. Determine how many people you're cooking for and purchase the right amount of ingredients based on your recipe instructions. When in doubt, buy extra. Check how much time the recipe *says* the preparation will take. Then give yourself an extra fifteen to thirty minutes.

Take your time. Give yourself a chance to practice. Don't get discouraged when julienning carrots is more difficult than it looks. Your first attempts won't be perfect. And as you challenge yourself more, you'll make more mistakes. But soon enough you'll be wowing your family with your culinary expertise. And as head chef, you're exempt from dishwashing duty!

33 Host a Presentation Night

You've made dozens of presentations for classes over the years. From plate tectonics to the mitochondria to the Battle of Yorktown, you probably know the Google Slides premade theme selector like the back of your hand at this point. But have you ever made a presentation voluntarily for someone you actually like? That's what a presentation night is for.

For the uninitiated, a presentation night involves a group of friends getting together to give informal presentations on any topic of their choice, from a definitive ranking of all the Pokémon generations to which wild animals you think you could beat in a one-on-one fight. The point is to create a unique, funny, and still somehow informative talk that'll make an impression on your friends. And presentations are a lot more fun to make when they're about something you care about. So gather your creatively inclined friends, set up the TV or projector, and hit Present.

How to Do It

Theme it. You can give your night any theme you want. It can be hyper-specific or extremely broad. Just make sure your friends are all on the same page.

Hone your topic. Aim to be witty, wacky, unexpected—calibrated to make your friends laugh as hard as possible. Try a topic along the lines of "Who in the Friend Group Would Die First in a Zombie Apocalypse: A Definitive Ranking" or "Bikini Bottom, a Class-Based Analysis." Look up some of the creative ideas people have come up with on social media if you find yourself struggling for inspiration.

Prep your presentation. Fill your slides with pictures, videos, and "informative" graphs. When the night comes, stock up on snacks, find a comfy spot to park everyone, take precautions against interruptions, and get presenting. Cheer on your friends when it's their turn and put on your best performance during yours. With the right group of friends, it'll be a night to remember.

TO FILM OR NOT TO FILM

Because this trend emerged on social media, it can be tempting to film the experience in hopes of becoming the next viral sensation. If that's cool with your friends, good, but don't feel obligated to perform for the camera. The point is to have fun, not create a viral moment. And make sure your friends are comfortable with the spotlight before posting anything publicly.

34 Learn a Martial Art

Some people become interested in martial arts because they want to be able to kick butt. But practicing martial arts can also be one of the best all-around workouts your body can get. Tai chi, karate, judo, kickboxing, and other forms of artful attack and defense will sharpen your mind and strengthen your body. As you gain an understanding of the philosophies behind your practice, you'll learn about the importance of calm, restraint, and balance in life. With great power comes great responsibility, and though you probably won't be taking out villains with your awesome techniques, you'll gain a new perspective on how to use your physical body.

How to Do It

Learn about your options. Gyms and martial arts studios offer classes for all skill levels. Observe some classes or attend a tournament to learn about the different disciplines. Tae kwon do emphasizes foot and fist maneuvers; jujitsu involves lots of grappling and throwing; hapkido focuses on channeling energy through circular motions and carefully coordinated punches. You can focus on the one that you think will be the best fit for you (or that looks the coolest).

Choose a discipline. Find an instructor with many years of teaching experience under their belt. They should have a solid understanding of both the physical and the philosophical aspects of the practice. And they should foster a welcoming and open environment in their studio. Go to a few classes to see if you like the vibe.

Stick with it. As you progress in your study, you'll have a chance to achieve a rank or earn a series of colored belts that indicate your skill level. Even if you aren't the most gifted student, the activity will be good for your physical and mental health. You may also bond with your teacher and your fellow students.

ENTER THE DRAGON

Martial arts master Bruce Lee popularized high-energy self-defense on the big screen in the 1970s, starring in *Fist of Fury* and other box office hits. Even though Lee died at at thirty-two, he paved the way for other on-screen martial artists such as Jackie Chan and Jet Li. Check out one of his classics such as *Fist of Fury, Enter the Dragon,* and *Return of the Dragon*.

35 Establish an Exercise Routine

Everyone's body is different. What works for your body may not work for someone else's, and vice versa. But getting some form of physical exercise on a regular basis is good for both your physical and your mental health.

You don't have to be freakishly athletic to enjoy the benefits of exercise. People of all shapes and ability levels can experience the joys of physical movement. Exercise can take many forms: weight lifting at a gym, jogging through a park, learning yoga, or playing basketball at the local YMCA. Establishing an exercise routine can increase your overall energy level, help you sleep better, and even improve your daily mood.

How to Do It

Pick an activity. What options are available near you—from a specialized training center to a park with a few pickleball courts? What seems fun? What's doable at a beginner level? Would you like to exercise by yourself, with friends, or both? If you're not keen to spring for a gym membership, you can look up body weight exercises to try at home or get a great cardio workout riding your bike to and from school. If you'd like company but don't have an interested friend or loved one to join you, see if there's a local club or meetup you can join.

Establish a routine. It can be hard to fit exercise into your life when you have so much else going on. Start by finding time for a new activity once a week, even if it's only for twenty minutes. You can gradually build up to longer or more frequent workouts as your schedule and your stamina allow.

Set reasonable goals. You may hope to run a mile in a certain time or bench-press a certain amount of weight. Or maybe you just want to feel more energized throughout the day. Celebrate every bit of progress toward that goal, not just achieving the goal itself. And try not to compare yourself to others, even if you walk into a gym and see nothing but toned towers of pure muscle. Remember, everyone was new to fitness at one point, and they're all too busy with their own workouts to pay much attention to you anyway.

Mix it up. To avoid getting bored, try new activities occasionally. Use a coupon for a Pilates class. Splurge on an afternoon at a rock-climbing facility. Hit up the community pool for a swim. Play lawn games in a friend's backyard. You don't have to do an activity constantly—or skillfully—to find it fun and invigorating.

STAY MOTIVATED

It's easy to fall out of a workout routine. You miss a day because of a test or a cold, and before you know it, six months have gone by. To stay motivated, task a friend with keeping you on track. You can also keep a fitness journal or download a fitness app to track your progress. There's no motivator like being able to see tangible progress laid out on a nice graph or table.

36 Enter a Sports Competition

Maybe sports aren't your calling. Maybe you've committed to a full season of practices and games every year since elementary school. Wherever you fall on that spectrum, participating in an athletic competition can be worthwhile. Wherever you place, you can feel pride for reaching outside of your comfort zone or pushing yourself to your limit.

How to Do It

Choose a sport. Enter a 5K. Sign up for a weekend-long volleyball tournament organized by your local parks and rec department. Join an amateur archery competition.

Find a competition. Search the internet for upcoming events in your area. (Companies such as Nike sponsor runs in cities across the country.) Or contact your city's parks and rec department or local amateur sports clubs for other organized competitions. Normally, events will be announced online months in advance.

Be realistic. It probably isn't wise to enter a marathon if the last time you ran more than a mile was in seventh-grade gym class. Set realistic goals for your ability level, such as a sub-twenty-five-minute 5K, or ten points in a game of pickup basketball.

Train. Adapt your regular exercise routine to prepare. You'd be shocked at how much easier a seven-minute mile gets after just a month of regular running.

Have fun. It's fine if you don't dominate the competition. The only person you should be comparing yourself to is you two months ago.

FIND THE RIGHT FUEL

What we eat has a huge effect on our bodies, so it's smart to maintain a balanced and hearty diet when you're training for an event. Try to eat plenty of protein to allow your body to properly rebuild and recover. Hydrate before, during, and after your workout.

37 Practice Mindfulness

High school is full of challenges: schoolwork, relationships, work, and important life decisions. Maybe you're feeling the pressure. Or maybe you've become so used to stress that you barely notice it until *one more thing* pushes you over the edge. Even when you feel totally on top of everything, the hectic pace of life can be draining.

A simple, semi-regular mindfulness practice can help you reset. Mindfulness simply means being present in your body and in the moment. There are all sorts of ways to do this, from breathwork to stretches to mantras. Mindfulness practices can reduce anxiety, boost your mood, and even help you concentrate.

You don't have to become a meditation expert. You don't have to take a class or invest in an app—though you certainly can. Mindfulness apps offer a vast variety of guided exercises and practices, from straightforward meditations to storytelling sessions. There's also an abundance of free mindfulness resources online. Some soothing music or a wholesome ASMR video can also be a backdrop to a self-guided meditation, unless you prefer silence. If you can clear even five minutes from your busy schedule, you can make them mindful minutes.

How to Do It

Take a beat. Find a quiet spot if you can. Get into a comfortable position if possible. Press Play on a guided meditation video or podcast segment, or on a playlist of your preferred background noise. Set a timer. Close your eyes. Maybe place a hand on your chest to help ground yourself.

Notice your body. Inhale and exhale slowly, focusing on the physical sensation. Pay attention to how it feels to exist in your body. Are your shoulders tense? Make a conscious effort to relax the muscles. Is your leg stiff? Try to shift to a more comfortable position. This won't magically cure aches and pains, but unclenching and stretching will still be helpful.

Let the thoughts go. Clearing your mind is easier said than done. As soon as you start to relax, an urgent reminder might pop into your head, or a nagging worry may surface. Remind yourself that you'll deal with it after your timer goes off. Visualize those thoughts drifting away for now. Refocus on your body, your breath, and the moment you're experiencing right now.

BREATHE EASY

Here's a simple breathing exercise you can do anytime, whether you need to steady your nerves before a test or wind down before bed:

1. Take a deep breath through your nose while counting to four.
2. Hold your breath for seven seconds.
3. Slowly exhale while counting to eight. Do this a few times.
4. Repeat a few times.

38 Determine Your Blood Type

You might vaguely recall covering blood types in a biology class—or you might not. But knowing your blood type is important in case you ever need to give blood or receive an emergency transfusion. Blood types must be compatible for a transfusion to be safe.

How to Do It

Sign up for a blood drive. You can perform a service to the community *and* find out your blood type. Find out if your school holds a regular blood drive. If not, suggest that the administration organize one or volunteer to help a club facilitate one. You'll need a parent to sign a release form. (There are age restrictions, and certain people can't donate blood for health reasons, so get the details from the folks running the drive.) If the drive is run by the Red Cross, you'll receive instructions on downloading the Blood Donor app. After your donation has been processed, the app will be updated with your donor profile, including blood type.

Ask your doctor. If you're unable to donate, you can request your blood be typed next time it's drawn for a checkup at the doctor's office.

Keep track. Record your blood type in a safe place and then learn the types of your immediate family members. It's good to have this information in case of an emergency.

THE MAGIC LETTERS

The antigens on the surface of your red blood cells determine your blood type, and each type can be either positive or negative. (No type is better or worse than another.) The four main groups are A, B, AB, and O. Here's a quick rundown:

- O is the universal donor. If you're an O, you can give to anyone but only receive blood from other O's.
- AB is the universal recipient. If you're an AB, you can get blood from anyone but only give to someone else who's AB.
- A and B types can give to their types (A or B) and to ABs and receive from their types (A or B) and O's.

39 Learn to Read Food Labels

Maintaining a balanced diet is helpful for your overall health. If you have food allergies or intolerances, it's especially vital to know what's in the food you're eating. Even if you don't have any diet restrictions, chances are someone you know does—or will eventually, since our food tolerances can shift over the course of our lives.

The US Food and Drug Administration requires that every food package comes with a Nutrition Facts label. Learning to read food labels can help us make informed decisions about what we eat. They show a complete list of ingredients, offer a suggested serving size, and tell us the amount of protein, carbs, fat, and vitamins we're getting in each serving.

How to Do It

Check the serving size. A food label lists a recommended serving size and the number of servings per container. Typical serving sizes are one cup of cereal, five pretzels, and two cookies. But come on—who only eats two cookies? Every person is unique, and everyone processes food differently. Always listen to your body and take all recommendations with a grain of salt.

Check the numbers. The label shows the number of calories, types of fat (trans fats typically yield no nutritional benefits, while unsaturated fats, like those found in avocados, do a body good), cholesterol, sugar, sodium, carbohydrates, and protein per serving. Amounts are given as a percentage of the total daily recommended intake, based on a two-thousand-calorie-per-day diet. But remember, these recommendations are based on averages. What may be a perfectly reasonable number of calories for one person to function throughout the day may be too much or not enough for someone else.

Consider vitamins. You'll also see percentages of vitamins and minerals, such as calcium and iron. These nutrients are measured in grams or milligrams. If it's all a bunch of zeroes in this section, you might not be getting many nutrients out of this food.

VITAL VITAMINS

Vitamins and minerals in foods can have health-boosting benefits. See if you can spot any of these on a food label:

- calcium
- dietary fiber
- iron
- potassium
- Vitamin D

40 Develop a Healthier Food Habit

You've probably been told to avoid junk food whenever possible, but you've also probably heard a million different takes on what junk food *is*. High in sugar, high in fat, ultra-processed? Here's the bottom line: All food is fine in moderation (barring allergies and severe intolerances). Life is too short not to eat that last doughnut. But if you find yourself struggling with the *moderation* part, you can make some adjustments.

If you feel a craving getting out of control, try gradually cutting back on how often you eat that particular treat, replacing it with an alternative as needed. If you'd like to shift your eating habits toward vegetarianism or veganism—or into omnivore territory if you've been on a plant-based diet—pick a few switches or additions to make to your food lineup.

How to Do It

Decide what change to make. Do you have trouble digesting more than a certain amount of a certain food? Do you find that you keep eating it even after you're full and then feel uncomfortable later? Has your doctor advised you to eat more greens to boost your iron levels? Make sure whatever change you're making won't significantly impact your nutritional intake. For instance, if you're minimizing red meat, load up on other sources of protein such as beans, fish, or soy products to keep your energy levels up.

Set goals. Sudden, extreme changes in your diet tend to do your body more harm than good. And denying yourself food when you're hungry is *very* unhealthy; it'll create more problems for your metabolism in the long term. Instead of cutting out a food entirely, try swapping some of it for something else. Instead of one more cookie, have some trail mix made of nuts and dried fruit. Instead of eating yet another salad, put some spinach in your go-to smoothie and blend it enough that you barely notice it.

Pay attention to your body. If you're feeling weak, irritable, fatigued, or scatterbrained, you may not be getting enough to eat. Don't be afraid to adjust your approach and your goals. The ultimate goal is to feel as good as possible, physically and mentally—not to check something off a checklist.

FAST FACTS

Fasting is popular in some wellness circles, but it shouldn't be taken lightly. Our bodies need proper nutrition and hydration to survive, and skimping on food can have serious repercussions. If you're considering fasting, talk to a doctor or nutritionist BEFORE you try it. And bear in mind that fasting is NOT a way to lose weight. Depriving your body of food will leave you with vitamin deficiencies, metabolic issues, and a whole host of problems you didn't bargain for.

41 Plant an Herb Garden

Since ancient times, herbs have been used for medicinal purposes—and cherished for their scents and flavors—all over the world. Herbs like caraway, oregano, and tarragon are commonly used in food. You may have had mint, lavender, or chamomile in an herbal tea. Growing your own herbs can be both easy and rewarding. With the right light, enough water, and some green-thumbed care, you can nurture them from seeds to sprouts in just a few weeks.

How to Do It

Prepare a spot. With proper treatment, herbs will grow indoors all year. You'll need at least some sunlight, but lots of herbs can grow in low or medium light exposure. If you have pets, find a place where you can keep your plants clear of curious paws and snouts. Add a small shelf to a wall or set them on top of a bookcase.

Assemble supplies. Shop around for several smallish planters or for pots placed in trays that will hold water. Look for containers that have good drainage. Put a thin layer of gravel in the bottom of each pot to help excess water drain. Buy the right kind of soil mix (ask the salesperson at the store or check online).

Gather seeds or cuttings. You can likely find seeds for sale at a local garden center, hardware store, or grocery store. It's also possible to order seeds online.

Or you can ask a gardening friend for a cutting from one of their already-thriving herbs. However you come by your herbs, choose. Some will thrive and others won't, so experiment with different types.

Plant! Put a few seeds in each pot, an inch or two (2.5 to 5 cm) under the soil. Place the pots near a window that gets sunlight from the south or west. Keep the soil moist, but don't overwater—once or twice a week should do. Within a couple of weeks, you'll start to see baby herbs poking out of the soil.

Use and maintain. Snip off a few leaves, run them under cold water, pat them dry, and add them to your meals. If plants such as basil start to flower, pinch the flower off to keep the plant growing more leaves.

A MEDLEY OF SCENTS AND FLAVORS

Try growing—and cooking with—these lesser-known herbs:

- **Anise** tastes tangy in salads as an herb and sweet in cookies in seed form.
- **Borage** tastes a bit like cucumber and is delicious in iced tea and lemonade.
- **Chervil** tastes similar to parsley and is perfect for soups.
- **Hyssop** has a pungent taste and can be mixed into onion dip.
- **Lovage** tastes similar to celery and is yummy in soups and salads.

42 Know Your Silhouette and Colors

Thanks to nonstop coverage of overstyled red carpet looks, endless trending "aesthetics" on social media, and influencers who always manage to look perfect (for the camera at least), fashion pervades our lives. Given how quickly trends move in the social media age (cottagecore? clean girl? coquette? Y2k?), it can feel like you're falling behind if you don't completely revamp your wardrobe every other month. The fashion industry thrives on these microtrends, pushing you to constantly reinvent your style—and constantly spend your hard-earned money on new clothes that will be obsolete by the end of the summer. But it doesn't have to be like this. Understanding the clothes and colors that flatter your specific shape and skin tone will help you to build a wardrobe that will last you years, saving you tons of money and cutting down on tons of waste.

How to Do It

Research your options. Search for silhouette illustrations, styling hacks, clothing recommendations, and makeover tips online.

Ask an expert. To figure out what colors look best on you, fashion experts look at your skin, eyes, and hair for complementary tones. One approach is to go to the mall and ask a professional to assess what colors are best for you. Some department stores and many cosmetic stores employ image consultants who love to talk about this stuff all day. If that doesn't work for you, look for some affirming stylists' accounts on social media.

Build your wardrobe. Look for sturdy, well-made clothes that will last years. Avoid fast-fashion brands that pollute the environment—and whose products disintegrate in three to five business days.

WHAT SEASON ARE YOU?

In the world of fashion, you'll sometimes hear people talk about what season they are. Beauty professionals use this concept to figure out what colors look best on people. Check out the graph below and see where you fall. Do you fit into more than one category? You're probably a mix of seasons—most people are.

SEASON	SKIN UNDERTONES	HAIR COLOR	EYE COLOR	COLORS THAT LOOK GOOD ON YOU
spring	warm undertones	blond, strawberry blond, or brown	blue, green, hazel, or brown	peach, yellow, golden brown
summer	cool undertones	blond or brown	blue, green, or gray	sea green, lavender, rose brown, soft blue
autumn	warm undertones	deep red or brown	green, hazel, or brown	beige, orange, gold, dark brown
winter	cool undertones	brown or black	gray, brown, or black	white, black, navy blue, red, bold pink

43 Learn About Safe Sex

Okay, you know the drill. If you're going to be intimate with someone during your teenage years (or later), you have to be safe about it. If you go to a school that provides ample safe sex education or have grown up in a family that talks openly about this topic, you may already be well prepared. But it's always possible to learn more.

Any kind of sex with any person comes with risks, from STDs to unwanted pregnancy. You should be familiar with various methods of birth control and how to access them. Do you know how to properly use a condom? Do you know how to give and ask for enthusiastic consent? Are you prepared to slow down or stop if either of you becomes uncomfortable or uncertain?

Sex doesn't have to be scary. Ask a lot of questions, educate yourself, and keep your body safe.

How to Do It

Talk to a reliable adult. Yes, bringing up sex with your parents can range from embarrassing to downright difficult, depending on your situation. But start there if you can. If parents are a no-go, talk to a doctor, a school nurse, or another knowledgeable and trustworthy adult.

Go to a clinic. If you have a primary care physician, they can offer you confidential guidance. Planned Parenthood is an affordable resource for basic information and health counseling.

Tread carefully online. There's tons of online content about sex. Look for reliable sources, such as the websites of reputable clinics or health agencies and qualified health professionals. Double-check any information you get online.

NO MEANS NO

Nobody should ever pressure somebody else into having sex. Period. Whether it's your first or fifth time, you are always allowed to say no. Even if you say yes and then change your mind, at any point and for any reason, you can stop. The same rule applies if the person you're with says no, at any point or for any reason. And don't forget that if someone is intoxicated in any way, they are unable to consent. So steer clear of any mind-inhibiting substances beforehand.

44 Get a Passport

Traveling outside of your own country is exciting and doesn't have to be life-changingly expensive. But it does require careful planning. And you won't get far without a passport! The little booklet contains your name, your place and date of birth, a unique identification number, and a photo of your face. Authorities check it at airports and border checkpoints when you enter another country. The passport proves you are who you say you are and lets the government keep tabs on people's comings and goings.

Even if you don't have an international trip planned in the near future, it's a good idea to get a passport now. It'll last ten years before it has to be renewed, and who knows what travel opportunities could come your way in the next decade?

How to Do It

Find a passport-processing location. This could be a dedicated passport office or your town's government center. Check if you can fill out any of the forms online to save time. See if your local office can take your photo there or if you have to bring an acceptable photo with you. You can get a passport photo professionally taken at some drugstores, retail stores, and mail delivery centers. It should be taken within the past six months and show your full face, eyes open with a neutral expression in front of a white or beige background.

Gather documents. Along with the photo, you'll need proof of identification and US citizenship. A birth certificate, driver's license, or other state-issued ID works best, but if you don't have access to any of these, check the government website for alternatives. If you're under eighteen, a parent or guardian will need to be present and provide consent. Total fees are around $130, and your passport should arrive within four to six weeks, or two to three weeks if you pay an additional expedited processing fee of $60.

Keep it safe. Store your passport in a safe place at home. When you travel, carry it in a small crossbody bag or a document pouch that you keep with you at all times. It's a pain to replace!

GETTING PAPERWORK IN ORDER

If you're not a US citizen, you can still look into what documentation you'll need for any kind of travel. Refresh yourself on what to say—and not say—if questioned by immigration authorities. Know your rights in case you're stopped.

45 Visit a Foreign Country

Traveling abroad certainly isn't something all teens have the opportunity to do, but you should jump at the chance if it comes along. Though *your* world of book reports and soccer practice can seem small sometimes, the real world is a massive, interconnected network of people living their own interesting and distinct lives. Traveling to another country can give you a new perspective on our beautiful mess of a planet and your place in it.

How to Do It

Use your connections. If you have any relatives living in other countries, see if they're open to hosting you. Your parents are much more likely to approve an international trip if they know a trustworthy adult will be watching out for you on the other side of the border or ocean. This could also be an opportunity to get in touch with your roots and explore your ancestral lands. Or if you have a pen pal in another country, ask if they're open to a visit.

Use programs. If you don't have a contact in another country, research international exchange and work programs. Find out as much as possible about the organization you'd like to go with, the host country you want to visit, the fees involved, and any scholarships offered.

Get parental buy-in. Present your well-researched plan to your parents. Emphasize how killer it looks on a college application to already have volunteering experience in another country as a teen. If you play your cards right, you could soon be exploring new terrain and having the adventure of a lifetime.

ANOTHER STATE OF MIND

If you're unable to travel internationally, plan a trip to another US state. Our nation is so huge and varied that going from the Midwest to California or from New York to the Deep South can be like stepping into a foreign country.

46 Learn a Foreign Language

If you aren't one of the millions of teens in this country who grew up speaking a language other than English, it's not too late to start catching up. Learning a foreign language is worth the time and effort, and you'll be glad you stuck with it past the *¿Què?* stage. More than one in five US residents speak a language other than English at home, so knowing another language can help you connect with peers. It can also make foreign travel much easier. Not to mention that it can look good on a college app!

How to Do It

Practice! Your school may have a second-language credit requirement. That's a good start, but you aren't going to become fluent by only practicing between ten and eleven every Tuesday and Thursday. Making language an extracurricular activity can help it to feel fun and less like homework. Pick one of the many apps or websites dedicated to making language learning fun and exciting. Practice with headphones at first, and don't be shy about repeating phrases aloud as you hear them.

Make it fun. Listening to music or watching a TV show in a foreign language (with subtitles at first) is a form of practice that doesn't feel like practice. It can also teach you common slang that you won't find in your textbook. If any of your friends are also keen to learn the language, practice with them.

Talk to native speakers. If you already know native speakers, hang out with those who are willing to point out your mistakes—and teach you fun words. Offer to swap lessons with someone who speaks the language you're studying and is learning English. If you don't have any IRL connections like this, try a website or app that connects you with native speakers. These sites allow each of you to practice conversation in the language you wish to learn.

SEIZE THE DAY

Some people decide they want to learn a foreign language later in life, but it's best not to wait. Once you leave high school, lessons get pricey and free time is harder to spare. It's also easier to pick up a language at sixteen than at twenty-six or thirty-six because of the way our brains develop.

"Oye Como Va"

47 Explore a New Cultural Tradition

Whether you realize it or not, you regularly take part in cultural traditions, both on special occasions and in your daily life. Some of those traditions may be handed down from relatives. Others are so commonly practiced you likely don't even register them as traditions (like doing the wave at a baseball game or setting off fireworks on July 4). But have you ever familiarized yourself with a new tradition from someone else's culture? Everywhere you look, there are tons of rituals and celebrations to appreciate, from Japanese tea ceremonies and lantern festivals to Tunisian henna art to Mexican Dia de los Muertos fiestas.

How to Do It

Educate yourself. Pay attention to how friends from various cultural backgrounds celebrate their homelands and histories—and to the daily customs their families practice that differ from yours. Express respectful interest in their practices. Don't demand that they educate you on their cultures, but encourage them to feel comfortable sharing these aspects of their lives with you.

Respectfully observe. Ask if they'd be willing to let you join a special gathering as a guest and observer. Jewish friends might invite you into their sukkah—a temporary, hand-built house—to eat a tasty dinner during Sukkot, a yearly harvest festival. Argentines like to share a cup of maté, an antioxidant-rich green tea drink that everyone sips from the same bombilla, or straw. Someone might show you a new recipe unique to their cultural heritage or a customary greeting they reserve for elders in their community.

Explore your community. Find cultural and community centers in your area, which often host events that are open to the public. Attend a festival or a holiday celebration. Or find an immigrant-owned restaurant and sample their menu.

YOU'RE NOT THE MAIN CHARACTER

When learning about a tradition outside of your own culture, remember that you're there to observe and appreciate as a guest. Don't try to actively participate in all aspects of the experience, especially if you're not fully familiar with their meaning and significance. You wouldn't want someone bursting into your birthday party and blowing out your candles for you, so don't do the same with others' celebrations. Besides, if you act like a buffoon, it'll reflect badly on whoever invited you.

48 Visit Your State Capital

You probably had to memorize all fifty state capitals back in grade school, but have you ever visited the political center of your own state? It may not be the most glamorous city (Sacramento instead of San Francisco? Albany instead of NYC?), but it's an important civic center. At the very least, it'll have some cool architecture, some interesting history, and a gift shop. Tour the capital closest to you. If you find it lacking in excitement, make it part of a bigger road trip where you can see more of what your state has to offer.

How to Do It

Get to the capital. Your school might sponsor a field trip to your local state capital, but you can also take it upon yourself to head there with family or friends. Pile in a car and drive, or see if you can get there on public transit.

Tour the capitol. Each capital-with-an-*a* has a capitol-with-an-*o*, a building or campus where your state's lawmakers meet. Check the city's website in advance to see if you need to arrange a tour of the capitol in advance. If you happen to see any legislators there, don't hesitate to talk to them about the issues facing you and your family. If they try to run away from hard questions, well, you'll be old enough to vote soon enough.

Check out the rest of the city. The capital's website will give you a sense of the city's main attractions. There may be a visitors' center where you can grab a map or brochure. Visit any historic sites, check out the biggest green space, and seek out some food you can't easily find in your hometown.

THE ULTIMATE CAPITAL

The capital is, of course, Washington, DC. Rife with political scandal and studded with monuments to long-dead presidents, DC is a great place to visit for a long weekend. It boasts dozens of free museums and a chance to see the Secret Service in action. Not to mention an entire city of 700,000 semi-enfranchised American citizens to explore. (DC has no voting representative in Congress, despite having a larger population than the entire state of Wyoming.)

49 Take a Camping Trip

Mix trekking through fields of wildflowers, bathing in an aquamarine lake, and sleeping under the stars with getting attacked by bloodthirsty mosquitoes, being forced to use leaves for toilet paper, and eating cold beans straight from the can, and you get the equally amazing and challenging experience of camping. Leaving behind creature comforts like your microwave and memory foam pillow can take some getting used to. But it's a small price to pay to become completely enveloped by the majesty of nature. Whether with relatives, friends, or a community group, camping for a few days will instill deep appreciation for natural splendor, survival skills, and your comfy bed back home.

How to Do It

Get ready. Your group should include one or two people who've camped before. Decide if you want to do car camping, stay in a cabin, or go for the full-on tent experience. Then thoroughly research the best spot for your outdoors excursion. Check that the weather is going to be reasonable for the time and place you are going. Camping in cold weather is not for the faint of heart!

Be prepared. Buy or borrow the supplies you'll need: a tent, a warm sleeping bag, plenty of food and water, insect repellent, some music (or, even better, instruments to play), flashlights with extra batteries, waterproof hiking shoes, rain gear, and sunscreen. Bring your phone and charger, but don't expect 5G service to reach you without fail in the wilderness.

Set up camp. Pick a spot to pitch your tent. Areas farther from the water are usually less laden with bugs, and locations surrounded by trees will protect you from wind and sun. Pitch your tent on dry, flat ground void of big rocks and anthills. Or if your tent has to be on slanted ground, position your head uphill.

PACK IT IN, PACK IT OUT

When camping, be sure to take out everything you brought in with you, including any granola bar wrappers, empty water bottles, and soiled clothing. When going number two in the woods, dig a small hole, do your business, and cover the hole. But never bury toilet paper, as it can take years to fully biodegrade. Research more eco-friendly cleaning methods for alternatives. If you must use it, put it in a secure plastic bag to dispose of once you're back in civilization.

50 Go for a Hike

Do you want to experience the joys of nature and physical exercise without having to sleep on the ground or bathe in a river? Going for a short day-hike accomplishes this with the promise of returning to your cushy bed when the day is over. You don't have to conquer Mount Everest for a rewarding experience. The point isn't to *conquer* nature at all—it's to become part of it. Communing with nature is a great way to bust out of your day-to-day slog and gain a new perspective on our beautiful, interconnected world. A good hike is just as much about the journey as the destination.

How to Do It

Gather a crew. Hikes are more fun and much safer when you go with friends or relatives, so recruit a companion or two to join you. Discuss the type of hike you want to go on. Make sure you're on the same page in terms of length and level of difficulty. You can download an app that lets you search for trails in your area; filter by length, difficulty, altitude, and more; and see user uploaded photos and reviews of trails, as well as downloadable maps.

Pack and prep. Bring a backpack with some basic provisions, and wear comfortable shoes. Learn how to recognize poison ivy, poison oak, and other problematic plants, and find out if any dangerous wildlife is known to roam the area. If you're entering bear territory, stay prepared with bear spray and a plan in case of a sighting.

Savor the moment. At the end of your hike, reward yourself with a nice rest and some quiet moments of contemplation. Then give yourself a pat on the back and head back toward civilization.

THERE AND BACK AGAIN

Here's what to pack for your hiking adventure:

- **Plenty of water.** It's easy to get dehydrated while walking, especially if the weather isn't hot enough to remind you to drink. Drink a bit of water before beginning the climb and sip along the way.
- **Snacks.** You'll work up quite an appetite during your trek. Sandwiches and trail mix are hiking staples for a reason.
- **Sunscreen.** Even if the weather isn't sunny, protect your skin. Reapply if you're outside longer than two hours.
- **A camera.** You probably keep one in your pocket at all times, but make sure it's handy to capture the beauty around you.

51 Learn the Constellations

Constellations are groups of stars that, when linked, form shapes in the night sky. Phoenicians dreamed up this connect-the-dots game some three thousand years ago. In the second century, the Greek astronomer Ptolemy further developed the concept and recorded forty-eight out of the eighty-eight constellations that we commonly recognize today. Constellations typically form easy-to-spot images of animals (lions, fish, and crabs), objects (scales and arrows), and mythological figures (Orion and Hercules). Learning the constellations turns looking at the night sky into a whole new experience. It can feel like reaching across time. You're looking up at the same sky as the ancient Phoenicians—tracing pictures in the stars, dreaming of what lies beyond our small place in the universe.

How to Do It

Keep your eyes peeled. Some constellations, such as Ursa Major (the Great Bear), Scorpius (the scorpion), or Orion (the hunter) are visible without a telescope or superstrong binoculars. If you live

THE BIG MISCONCEPTION

The Big Dipper, which most people think of as one of the big-time constellations, isn't a constellation at all. It's an asterism, or a nonofficial grouping of stars with a popular name. Who knew stars had to deal with social hierarchies too?

in an area without much light pollution, check the forecast and pick a clear night to camp out in someone's backyard. If you live in or near a city, plan a visit to a more remote area for a better view of the cosmos.

Access the tech. Barring an unexpected trip on the next NASA flight, the best way to study the constellations is through a high-powered telescope. Visit a planetarium to get access to some high-tech equipment or order an amateur stargazing kit online.

Read the heavens. Stargazing apps can help you identify constellations. Once you establish a few signposts and a sense of interstellar direction, the sky's the limit.

CONSTELLATIONS AND HOROSCOPES

You may have noticed that the twelve zodiac signs share their names with constellations. The same way that countries are located at specific coordinates on lines of latitude and longitude, stars are located at coordinates along lines of right ascension and declination on what's referred to as the celestial sphere. Like lines of longitude and latitude, coordinates on the celestial sphere are interpreted in degrees—but they also represent periods of time. For example, the coordinates of the constellation Scorpius, known as Scorpio in astrology, correspond to a space in the night sky that spans from about October 24 to about November 21. Everyone's birthday falls somewhere in the night sky, and that determines your zodiac sign.

52 Make a Podcast

How many times have you heard the phrase "You *have* to check out this true crime podcast"? Podcasting is a booming industry, with millions of people around the world producing hours and hours of content every day. Why not try your hand at it? Your show doesn't have to cover disemboweled corpses and vicious serial killers (unless that's your thing). It can be about anything under the sun.

Of course, some podcasts make money—big money. But most don't. If you think of this as an exercise in self-expression instead of a potential business venture, it'll be more rewarding and fun.

How to Do It

Choose a premise. Decide what your show will be about. You can take a research-centric approach, such as telling weird tales from history with your own scripted commentary. You can aim to interview guests, such as up-and-coming artists from your community. Or you can keep it loose and informal: just you and your friends riffing about a topic that interests you. Make sure your show has some sort of outlined structure to avoid awkward pauses and never-ending rants.

Choose a format. Decide whether you want your podcast to be filmed or audio only. Putting a face behind the voice of your show can be great for attracting new listeners, but having to be in front of a camera adds another layer of stress to your performance. Download simple, free podcasting software and teach yourself the basics. Invest in a microphone and headphones if you want improved sound quality. Or just record on your phone for low-fi results.

Share your show. Upload episodes to YouTube, or take some additional steps to get it on streaming services for free. Use social media to promote your show. Podcast clips go viral all the time, so it doesn't hurt to snip some key moments from each episode and upload them to a dedicated profile.

THE PODCASTER'S TOOLBOX

Here's some equipment that'll help you on your podcasting journey:

- a decent-quality microphone
- a digital camera (or your phone) if your show will be filmed
- audio recording software; Audacity is a free and robust option that also allows you to edit your product
- a quiet space to record

53 Keep a Scrapbook

Do you hold on to birthday cards, movie ticket stubs, love letters, photo booth prints, and other nostalgic mementos? If your desk is overflowing with keepsakes or the "junk box" under your bed is no longer fitting *under* your bed, it's time to get more creative with your organizing. Try using a scrapbook to store the small (and flat) material things that matter to you. It can be a constantly evolving collection of items that work together to tell the unique story of your life. Plus it can give you an entertaining experience in artful organization.

How to Do It

Get the book. Shop around for a blank notebook or album. Use light-colored pages if you want to write on them in dark ink, or black pages if you want to use silver or other light-colored pens (or if you're going for a goth look). Also pick up glue, tape, stickers, ribbons, and other decorative items to add flair.

Put it together. Sit at a clean workspace and organize your items chronologically or by theme. Think of each page as an individual work of art. Mix and match different elements, such as photos, play programs, newspaper clippings, and artwork given to you by friends.

Preserve details. Label the pages with dates, names, and locations so you'll always know who went with you to that concert (write the person's name under the ticket) or how old you were when you had your appendix taken out.

A SCRAPBOOK SERIES

If you have tons of stuff, keep a series of scrapbooks, each one dedicated to a particular time period or a particular area of your life—one for school-related stuff, one for crush memorabilia, another for music tickets and concert pics, and so on.

54 Make a Video

You may have already made a few short-form videos for TikTok or YouTube. Maybe you've even amassed a bit of a following with mukbangs or try-on hauls. But have you learned the ins and outs of high-quality video production? We've all got powerful cameras in our pockets and are inundated with tools for simple video making. But if all we know how to use are simple tools, we're only produce simple videos. Challenge yourself to create a high-quality, carefully constructed video that you'd be proud to showcase.

How to Do It

Develop your vision. Decide what kind of video you want to make. Be ambitious, but not too ambitious. You're not going to create a feature-length film right away. Do you want to make a vlog? A dramatic short film? A hilarious sketch? What about a thoroughly researched video essay on a topic that fascinates you? If you don't know where to start, search through YouTube for inspiration.

Use the right equipment. To up your production quality, invest in a digital camera and a professional microphone, or rent them from your local library.

Edit your creation. Get some free editing software and teach yourself to use it. Watch some in-depth YouTube tutorials if reading the user manual is making your eyes glaze over.

Share! Show your completed video to close friends and family and ask for honest feedback. Use any constructive criticism to improve your craft. If you want the world to see your masterpiece, upload it to YouTube. Just remember to always be safe when making public-facing content. Never upload anything too personal or incriminating.

STREAMING SENSATION

You could try live streaming on Twitch or YouTube. Stream yourself playing video games, painting, or just hanging out. Remember that when you're live, you can't edit the content, so be careful not to say anything you shouldn't.

55 Learn Music Production

Back in the day, DJs carted around backbreaking crates of vinyl records to block, house, and underground parties to spin hours-long custom-made mixes. Though some DJs still swear by vinyl, modern music production technology means you only need a laptop and a creative mind to produce music of your own. Whether you want to make trap beats, dance pop, or EDM, learning music production from the comfort of your room has never been easier. There's a reason we have a whole genre called *bedroom* pop.

How to Do It

Pick a DAW. Decide on a digital audio workstation that works for you. Your DAW will be your one-stop shop from the first step of production to the final mix. You could go with a free program such as GarageBand or spring for a pricier but more robust option such as FL Studio or Ableton.

Learn the program. After installing your DAW, you may be intimidated when you open it and see what looks like a NASA-worthy array of buttons, switches, and sliders. While it may seem overwhelming at first, with a little practice you'll get to know the program. Search beginner tutorials on YouTube and slowly work your way up to more advanced stuff.

Make the music. Look up tips for producing your musical style of choice (What's the perfect trap hi-hat? How do I EQ reverb on my indie rock banger?). Soon you'll be comfortable enough to start experimenting, crafting you own blend of styles and genres, and creating your unique musical identity.

SAILING THE SEVEN SEAS

Digital audio workstations are expensive. It can be tempting to search through shady websites for free pirated copies of a program. But be aware that these companies use extremely vigorous license tracking. If they catch you using pirated software, they retain the right to take down any music you've posted online.

56 Create a Comic Strip

Back in the 1950s, adults were convinced that comic books would be the downfall of society. US congressional hearings cited comic books as a cause for rising juvenile delinquency. Americans worried that the violent adventures of Flash, Wonder Woman, and Batman would corrupt impressionable teenagers and distract them from more important things, such as doing homework and drinking lots of milk. Today, however, comic books and cartoon strips are recognized as important art forms. From Western classics like *Peanuts* and *Superman* to incredible serialized Japanese manga like *One Piece* and *Berserk*, the world of comics has never been more exciting to explore. Taking inspiration from your favorites, try creating an original comic book or cartoon strip.

How to Do It

Choose a theme, style, and tone. You can make serious social statements, indulge your surreal sense of humor, or reveal personal perspectives on life.

Create characters. Come up with a cast to populate your strips. Are they humans, aliens, superheroes, or animals? All of them together in your own original *Dragon Ball*? What are their main personality traits? What role does each play in the world of the story?

Choose a format. You can create a few short panels, like an old-school newspaper comic strip, or a longer story told over dozens of pages. You can draw it the old-fashioned way with a pen, paper, and notebook, or you can use a tablet.

SUBSTANCE OVER STYLE

Don't worry if drawing isn't your strong suit. Being funny and charging your comics with unexpected emotion are more important than making everything look lifelike. If you're really struggling with the technical elements, consider partnering with a friend who excels at drawing. They can oversee the artwork while you focus on character, story, and text.

57 Take an Art Class

Personal expression and the arts go hand in hand. With the right tools and some patience, you'll find that even rudimentary skills can be honed to create something you can take pride in. Taking an art class is a wonderful way to tap into your creative instincts.

How to Do It

Find a class. Search online for art courses at a local school or community center. You should be able to take a multi-session course for no more than a few hundred dollars (though you might have to spend extra on supplies). If the enrollment fee is an issue, ask the instructor if scholarships or discounts are available.

Choose an art form. From figure drawing, pottery, and glassblowing to candle making, photography, and collage, you can find something that meshes well with your creative style.

Apply yourself. Pay close attention to your instructor, and don't take constructive criticism personally. Sure, no one wants to hear that their shading needs work, but it's probably true. You don't need to be great (or even good!) at your chosen art—but through patience and hard work, you can improve enough to take pride in your creations.

DIGITAL TEACHING

Nothing compares to hands-on instruction from a dedicated teacher, but online art tutorials can also improve your craft. If no in-person classes are available in your area, check online for instructors who teach remote courses via video conferencing. Of course, social media is full of self-proclaimed experts (and some actual experts!) sharing everything from step-by-step instructions to general principles to ultra-specific tips on all kinds of art forms—for free. Just make sure you find a few influencers who are truly qualified practitioners before you plunge in.

58 Learn to Play an Instrument

You might already play the saxophone in your school band or the viola in a community orchestra. But even if you don't participate in any extracurricular musical activities, it isn't too late to pick up the skill. In fact, it's much easier to pick up music as a hobby now than it will be later in life. Sheet music, complex technique, and indecipherable jargon can seem daunting at first, but don't be deterred. The rewards of knowing how to shred the guitar or improvise an impeccable solo will far outweigh the frustration of your first few lessons.

How to Do It

Pick an instrument. If you're into heavy, thrashing hardcore punk, try picking up the guitar or drums. If romantic-era classical is more your style, try the violin or piano. You don't necessarily need to own the instrument you're learning. Some music centers offer rental options, and some instructors provide instruments to play during lessons.

Get lessons. Check online for local offerings of private lessons. If one-on-one sessions with a professional musician are too pricey, that's okay. Some of the greatest musicians of all time, from Jimi Hendrix to Louis Armstrong, were self-taught. Follow along with online tutorials and play along with your favorite songs over and over.

Practice. Practicing is the only way to improve. Make it fun by learning your favorite songs on your instrument, but don't forget to also practice the essentials: scales, technique, and playing along to a metronome. They may not be the most exciting activities in the world, but they make up the building blocks of musical expertise. With a little effort and enough time, you'll be shredding that cello soon enough.

INSTRUMENTS TO INVESTIGATE

If you think the violin and cello sound boring, check out one of these more unusual options.

- **Sousaphone:** This seriously heavy, giant horn circles the player's upper body and ends in a big bell that extends above the player's head. It's originally from the US and is mostly played in marching bands.
- **Timpani:** It's an Italian-born copper or brass bowl with calfskin or plastic stretched across its surface. When beaten, it makes a dramatic sound that builds to a big musical climax.
- **Zither:** This shallow, armless guitar from Europe has about forty strings and is plucked with a pick worn around the thumb. There are different types of zithers, including the dulcimer, which is often used in folk and bluegrass music.

59 Take a Dance Class

Sure, maybe you're willing to bust a move when you're blasting a playlist alone in your room. But do you have the confidence to dance in public? The best way to feel footloose the next time you step out on the dance floor—whether it be at a party or at prom—is to take a dance class. You can explore all sorts of styles, from hip-hop to modern to jazz. Pros at dance studios can show you the basics of artistic movement. Dancing is a fun way to exercise, get in touch with your body, and express yourself through movement.

How to Do It

Take a class. Studios and community centers offer classes for all levels of expertise, from beginner to advanced. Scan schedules online and email the instructor to determine which class is right for you. Don't be afraid if you're an amateur—in a beginner class, everyone is on the same page. A good teacher will be able to coach you through your initial clumsiness.

Use online resources. If practicing in public isn't the thing for you, find a course or free instructional video online. Famous choreographers who've worked with the world's greatest dancers have created videos that break down showstopping moves for the rest of us.

Bring the right gear. Different types of dance require different types of shoes—or no shoes at all—so lace up or lace down accordingly. Wear comfortable clothing that's loose but not likely to trip you up. Keep long hair tied back, and have a water bottle on hand.

SWING IS THE THING

In the 1930s and '40s, young people were jitterbugging to big-band tunes, throwing their partners high in the air, and coming up with radical choreography that still hasn't gone out of style. To catch up on your jump and jive, watch the dance numbers in the movie *Swing Kids* (1993) or see the Marx Brothers film *A Day at the Races* (1937), which has one of the most influential Lindy Hop sequences ever filmed. Classic Cab Calloway and Benny Goodman tunes are also worth checking out.

60 Participate in a Performance

Performing in a play might sound terrifying, but there's nothing quite like the thrill of seeing the curtain rise and stepping up to center stage for your first scene. It's an amazing feeling to slip into character and become someone else for a couple of hours. No matter how big or small your role is, give it your all and discover the joys of the stage.

How to Do It

Start at school. If your school has a drama department, try out for the next production. Find out the rehearsal and performance schedule ahead of time and make sure you can commit to it. If you can access the script before auditions, read it. (Or watch a film adaptation if one exists.) Audition for several parts if that's allowed. Don't be discouraged if you don't land a big role on your first try. Even the smallest roles can be tons of fun and crucial for a production.

Know the scene. Attend a community theater performance to familiarize yourself with the venue. Check online to see if they're holding auditions for any upcoming productions. Small theaters are often in search of good actors to fill kid and teen roles. It can be extra fun to act around adults who know the ropes and can offer you advice. Despite lacking the budget and prestige of

Broadway professionals, community theater productions are often polished and provocative. And by polished, we mean you should be ready for hours of rigorous rehearsal if you get cast.

Practice. If you have lines, practice them whenever you have a chance: on the way to school, while you're brushing your teeth, during a workout. Put every rehearsal and performance in your calendar app so you can show up on time and not double-book yourself. Take your cues from the director, the stage manager, and the more experienced actors. Be friendly to the stage crew, the costume and makeup team, the sound crew, and anyone else involved with the production.

BEHIND THE SCENES

If you're into theater but don't see yourself thriving under the spotlight, get involved behind the scenes. Volunteer to paint the backdrops, rig the lights, manage the stage, or help with costumes and makeup. If you're a musician, try out for the pit orchestra; you'll provide live music for productions, often from underneath the stage.

61 Write Your Manifesto

If you had to sum up your view on the meaning of life in a five-paragraph essay, what would you say? Have you ever attempted to refine your thoughts on the world into a clear, concise piece of writing? Now's a perfect time to do it. Your head is probably swimming with opinions on everything from your town's infrastructure to national politics to the tragic discontinuation of the Taco Bell Quesarito. A manifesto is a statement of belief that can be motivational, brutally honest, or hilariously satirical. Whatever your approach, a manifesto shines with solid concepts, clear communication, and an intent to sway readers' opinions.

How to Do It

Brainstorm. What do you feel strongly about? Your manifesto doesn't necessarily need to focus on a "serious" topic—it just needs to be serious to *you*. You might be passionate about the lack of disability accommodations at your school or the importance of protecting marginalized people in your community or the unnecessary fees tacked on to already expensive concert tickets.

Draft. After you've picked your topic, shape your opinion and outrage into a concise essay. Don't let it run too long lest you lose the interest of your audience. But don't make it so brief that you overlook crucial details.

Distribute. Share your manifesto on a secure social media profile or as a physical flyer. You can hand out your manifesto anywhere, but it's best to ask permission before taping a copy to every open surface in your school.

MANIFESTING THE FUTURE

Some of the world's most famous manifestos have described what a fairer, better world could look like. Unfortunately, the term has also been applied to some of history's most hateful and deluded rants. The right kind of manifesto is tethered to reality while imagining a future that's more fulfilling for everyone.

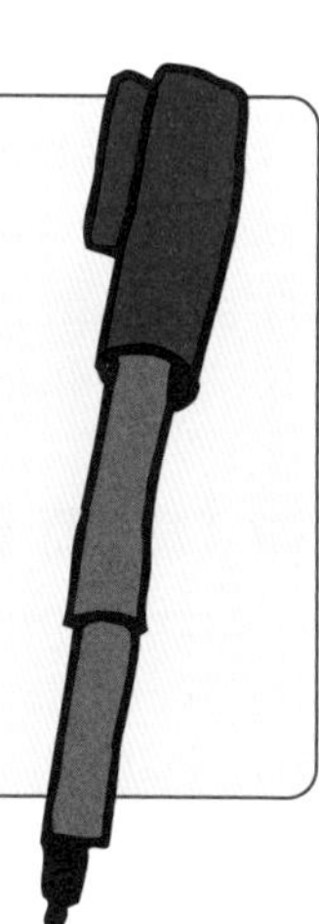

62 Make Your Own Halloween Costume

Some adults may tell you that you're too old for trick-or-treating now. But you're never too old to play dress-up. Halloween is the perfect excuse to let your creativity shine with a carefully tailored costume. Instead of shopping for a cheap-looking getup at the usual Halloween supply store where options are severely limited (one more police officer/prisoner couple's costume and we're gonna barf), celebrate the holiday by making your own costume.

How to Do It

Have a concept in mind. Pick a conceptual outfit or aim to cosplay as a specific character. If you find yourself struggling for inspiration, search social media for creative and unexpected costume ideas.

Assemble your outfit. Challenge yourself to assemble all the costume elements without resorting to ordering premade costume pieces online. It's better for the environment as well as your wallet. Raid thrift stores or your parents' closet for clothing items and accessories. Then break out the crafting supplies. Use fabric scraps, body makeup, paints, masks, and props to turn yourself into anything under the sun.

Debut your look. Attend or host a Halloween party. Make sure to take photos, whether you share them on social media or just keep them for your own collection.

THE MORE THE MERRIER

Recruit some friends and design your costumes as a group. You can be anything from Powerpuff Girls to hobbits to colorful cereal mascots. Choose a night a few days before Halloween where you all get together and create the costumes. Art is more fun as a group activity, and you can iron out any problems with your designs together before the big day.

63 Design a T-Shirt

Why spend thirty bucks or more on a trendy, massproduced T-shirt that will be worn by everyone you know and then go out of style in two months? Resist the homogenization of American fashion by customizing a crewneck. In a crowd of Shein queens and TikTok trend hoppers, you'll stand out as the stylistic visionary you are.

How to Do It

Get your canvas. Buy a solid-colored, blank T-shirt online or at an outlet store. Think of the shirt as a canvas for you to express your artistic visions.

Customize. Iron-on decals, patches, and band logos are fun options. Don't feel constrained to the standard image-across-the-chest look. Experiment with different places for your decal, like down the side seam or across the back. If you're an artist with a message, proclaim it proudly with vinyl lettering. You can embroider the shoulder-blade area with a sprawling floral cluster or cut slash marks across the back or sleeves for a punk-inspired look. Remember to use paints and markers that are permanent and specifically designed to be washed.

Scale it up. If you've got a little extra money, consider buying a small, personal screen-printing machine. That way, if your custom shirts are a hit, you can offer to make more for others to wear. Before you know it, you might be a DIY fashion entrepreneur.

ONLINE DESIGN

If you can afford a pricier option than the DIY method, some online stores let you create a custom T-shirt design on their web page and have it printed and shipped to you. Look for a site that uses ethically-sourced, fair-trade shirts.

64 Write a Real Letter

Given how digitized our social lives have become, it can sometimes seem like communication has lost some of its human touch. Even the most heartfelt, well-thought-out message becomes a mere series of 1s and 0s as you tap the Send button. Wouldn't it be great to have something you can hold? A physical reminder of a special relationship?

Pen-and-paper writing may seem archaic and time-consuming when compared with the instant gratification of online messaging, but there's something magical about pouring your soul into a letter, mailing it off, and waiting anxiously to hear back. Compared to typing, the act of writing is a slower, more deliberate process that forces us to consider every word. You can create a sentimental keepsake that may even make it into the recipient's scrapbook.

How to Do It

Select stationery. The paper you use should set the tone and convey your intention. Quality Japanese stationery is perfect for expressing thanks to a friend, while crisp white paper (possibly monogrammed with your initials) adds an air of sophistication to business-related letters.

Pick a pen. Your writing utensil should be comfortable to hold, have an ink color you like, and write clearly and steadily.

Write. Draft your letter on your phone, on a computer, or on a scrap piece of paper with a pencil. (It doesn't hurt to practice the physical act of writing.) Then copy the text onto your stationery with your pen. Use your best handwriting, but don't worry if it doesn't look perfect.

Personalize. If you're catching up with your long-lost friend from across the country, share a couple of printed photos to show what you look like these days. Writing to an object of your affection? Scent the letter with a small spray of perfume and seal the envelope with melted wax for extra drama.

Make a special delivery. Get the right stamp for your envelope's size and type. Address it to your lucky recipient and stick your missive in the mailbox. Or hand-deliver it if you'll be seeing the addressee in person.

THE WRITE STUFF

After you've drafted your letter, double-check it for egregious spelling mistakes and revealing asides. It's great to be candid and forthright with your letter recipient, but don't get carried away and spill your guts to the wrong person.

65 Write a Letter to Your Future Self

Who you are now indicates so much about who you'll be in the future. Yet as the years pass, some of your interests and perspectives will shift, and you'll develop new quirks, priorities, and outlooks. That's why it's cool to send a note to your future self. Upon receiving this epistolary surprise sometime in the middle of the twenty-first century, the grown-up version of you will thank your teenage self for taking an hour or so to record your hopes and dreams during your high school years. And you'll be able to reflect on how much you've evolved as time has gone by.

How to Do It

Take care of basics. Using pen and paper, or typing on a computer if you prefer, head your letter "Dear [Self]" and note the date.

Share your story. Write down what you want your adult self to remember about being the age you are right now. Imagine if you had to sum up all your journal entries in a few paragraphs. What would stand out as the most meaningful parts of your life and personality? Your favorite school subjects? Your best friends and worst enemies? Your current obsessions and hobbies?

Set it aside. Seal the letter in an envelope and stash it in a box of memorabilia that you'll be sure to keep (with your yearbooks or scrapbooks, for example). Years from now, you'll find it and savor the memories.

EMAIL TIME CAPSULE

Some websites allow you to upload a letter and choose a set date to have it sent back to your email account—say, ten years from now. That's a long time to not forget your password, but it's no less foolproof than, say, burying a box in a rented backyard.

66 Create a Tasty Dessert

What does whipping up a batch of oatmeal raisin cookies have to do with personal expression? Food is a universal human language, with recipes being handed down from generation to generation and bridging all sorts of geographical and cultural distances. Pulling a steaming-hot apple pie out of the oven or putting the finishing touches on a beautiful German chocolate cake can be just as rewarding as finishing a painting—not to mention tastier. Even if your desserts aren't going to earn any Michelin stars, you'll enjoy learning the art of baking, challenging yourself to improve, and eating the fruits of your labor.

How to Do It

Know the basics. Many desserts can be broken down into some combination of flour, sugar, and butter. Scan cookbooks and recipe sites for tried-and-true recipes you can master and then improve upon. Even a classic chocolate chip cookie can be transformed with a pinch of nutmeg or a sprinkle of cinnamon.

Get adventurous. If you're ready to journey further off the beaten path, try specialty cookbooks or sites. Experiment with ingredients you haven't used as often. Coconut, fruit juice, chutney, olive oil, dried fruits, spices—the possibilities are endless.

Try healthier substitutions. Agave nectar, which doesn't cause blood sugar levels to spike, can replace granulated sugar. Enriched white flour can be swapped out for whole wheat flour.

Embrace trial and error. Baking can be a finicky science, so accept that you're going to make mistakes. Any misfires are learning experiences you can apply to your next batch. Build in time for do-overs and a thorough kitchen cleaning at the end of your experiments.

DON'T PREMATURELY PREHEAT

Often, recipes instruct you to preheat the oven even before you've collected the ingredients, much less mixed them up. But novice bakers need extra time to read the recipe, measure, mix, and pour. To prevent your kitchen from heating up too fast (and to keep your energy bills down), give yourself adequate time to prepare before switching on the oven.

67 Volunteer for a Nonprofit Organization

Big businesses exist solely to produce money for their shareholders. Sure, they provide goods and services for consumers, but the goals of all mega companies are to take your hard-earned money and put it in the pockets of wealthy investors. By contrast, nonprofit organizations provide social and artistic services: raising money for the education of disadvantaged kids, hosting independent film festivals, representing the legal needs of refugees and immigrants, finding homes for stray animals. They're largely funded by donations and don't make decisions solely to increase revenue.

Volunteering for a nonprofit is a great way to 1) gain job experience in fundraising, project management, and public relations, 2) meet local leaders, scientists, and/or artists, and 3) give back to your community.

How to Do It

Find an org. Match your interests to a nonprofit group working in that field. If you're into art history, contact the nearest art museum and volunteer to lead exhibition tours. Love spending time outdoors? Find out if the local nature conservancy or botanical park needs someone handy with a leaf blower. If you're a math whiz, consider tutoring younger students at a nonprofit education center or after-school program. Are you good with your hands? Work with a nonprofit that constructs affordable housing.

Donate your time. Nonprofits are thrilled to work with volunteers on either a one-time or an ongoing basis. If you choose the latter, establish a schedule with the organization's project manager and stick to it. (College application offices and future employers will be impressed to see regular volunteering hours on your résumé.)

LOOK BEFORE YOU LEAP

Make sure you're clear on expectations before you make a commitment. Here are some questions to ask:

- What training will you receive?
- Who will supervise your work?
- Is there a minimum number of hours per month volunteers must commit to?
- What perks might you receive as a volunteer (tickets to events, networking opportunities)?
- If your school agrees, can you receive academic credit for volunteering?

68 Become Environmentally Conscious

Despite what certain figures in media and politics might try to tell us, the planet is heating up at an unprecedented rate, with dire consequences for the planet. The blame for this mostly falls on huge, polluting corporations that skirt guidelines and lean on politicians not to pass regulations. They sacrifice our futures for short-term monetary gain. So what can you do about it?

One way to combat climate change is to vote for politicians who take it seriously. You can also participate in demonstrations or contact your local officials, urging them to curb carbon emissions. There are also a few easy lifestyle changes you can make to decrease your personal carbon footprint. By doing this, you can make a small but direct contribution to a more sustainable future.

How to Do It

Recycle materials. Paper, cans, bottles, and certain plastics can all be recycled. Recycling saves overflowing landfills from millions of tons of garbage per year. That means less land pollution, more open space for parks, less soil and water pollution (which builds up when trash is buried) and less air pollution from trash being burned. Many city sanitation departments provide free recycle bins and regular collection service. If that's not the case where you live, take your recyclables to the nearest recycling center.

Compost food. Rather than throw away food scraps, toss them into a compost heap so they turn into fertilizer. If your community doesn't provide compost collection, you can do your own composting in a yard or a community garden plot. Check online for detailed instructions.

Minimize plastic. Avoid buying single-use plastic when possible. For example, invest in a reusable water bottle rather than relying on disposable plastic ones.

Reuse bags. Most plastic bags aren't biodegradable or recyclable. Buy a few sturdy bags to use for grocery runs and other shopping trips.

Reduce energy consumption. Most of our electric power comes from fossil fuels, which spew carbon dioxide into the environment and cause climate change. Reduce your fossil fuel consumption by turning off lights when you leave a room, unplugging devices when they're not being used, and adjusting the thermostat by a degree or two. To travel short distances, take public transportation, walk, or bike instead of driving whenever possible.

CLIMATE HISTORY

Scientists have been ringing alarm bells on climate change for a long time. Swedish chemist Svante Arrhenius predicted way back in 1896 that human activity related to greenhouse gas emissions would significantly impact the climate.

69 Contribute to Community Beautification

We're still a long way off from colonizing Mars, so chances are you're going to be stuck on Earth for the remainder of your life. Why not do everything you can to nurture this amazing yet fragile planet? You don't have to clean up an entire continent, but you can take pride in your immediate surroundings. There are countless small but impactful ways to make your neighborhood more beautiful.

How to Do It

Avoid littering. No one wants to see trash on the sidewalk or in parking lots. Littering also comes with a hefty fine if you're caught, so stick that candy wrapper in your pocket until you find a trash can.

Clean up trash. To combat litter buildup in your community, venture outside with a few plastic bags, rubber gloves, and a handheld trash picker. Pick up empty cans and fast-food bags at a local park or a busy intersection.

Plan and plant for the future. Volunteer with your local parks department to plant trees and flowers in sidewalk plots or to slap a new coat of paint on the park's benches. Working with the transportation department, you can adopt a bus shelter, painting and tidying it as needed. To add art to the cityscape, organize a mural painting on a blah exterior wall (after checking in with the building's owner). Look into joining or starting a community garden.

CHANGE BEGINS AT HOME

Could your house use a little beautification? That can start with you. Keep your yard clean, clear clutter from tables and floors, and persuade your family to start a garden or an indoor mini-conservatory.

70 Contact Your Local Officials

You might not be old enough to vote, but you can still get involved in public policy by expressing your opinions to local lawmakers. Local officials, such as your city's mayor and your district's supervisor, are supposed to represent community members. In other words, they work for *you*. You can push them to make positive change and responsible decisions. Make an appointment to meet with local representatives to make your voice heard.

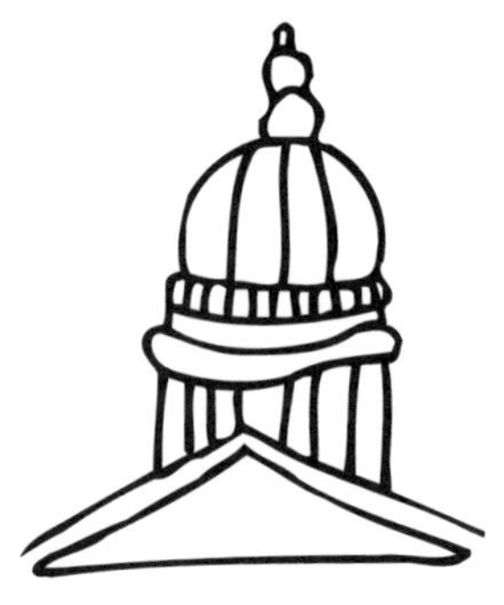

How to Do It

Identify an issue. Make a list of problems or concerns facing your community, like the increasing cost of living, out-of-control college tuition, and making birth control and safe sex information more accessible at school. Rank them in order of their importance to you, so that you can prioritize them when you have limited time to express your opinion.

Make an appointment. Do research to learn which officials make decisions about the topics that matter to you. Find their contact information on your local government's website. Call or email to request an appointment. Be polite.

Frame yourself as a caring citizen who wants to discuss a few concerns with your elected officials.

Be patient. Your message will probably end up at the desk of an assistant or intern. These folks are busy, so it may be weeks or even months until you can get in to see them.

Come prepared. When you do snag an appointment, it's less likely to be a leisurely sit-down meeting than a ten-minute window. So come prepared and don't dally over small talk.

Attend a meeting. If a one-on-one appointment doesn't pan out, many government meetings are open to the public. You may be able to voice a concern or opinion as part of a public comment session during a meeting.

PEOPLE HAVE THE POWER

If you can't get an exclusive visit with a legislator, send your thoughts in writing. For the biggest impact, encourage friends and classmates to do the same—the more emails, letters, or postcards you all send, the more attention you'll bring to the issue.

71 Join a Political Campaign

If you have strong opinions about policies in your community—or country for that matter—you can get more involved by joining a political campaign. Even though you may not be able to vote yet, your opinions are important. Don't leave all the decision-making to older generations. The decisions politicians make today will have significant impacts on *your* future, long after *they* have checked out of this mortal plane. Volunteering for an issue or a candidate that stirs your passion puts you in the driver's seat of your future.

How to Do It

Research candidates. General elections are held in early November. Primary elections for specific parties happen earlier in the year. Find out when your next election is and who's running. Check their websites for their stated policy proposals and priorities. You can also learn about candidates through local news interviews and profiles, or through statements they make at public meetings and candidate debates. Decide who aligns most with your personal views.

Volunteer. Contact campaign headquarters and find out how you can help. For a larger campaign, such as a senatorial or even presidential race, reach out to the local chapter of your candidate's campaign.

Show up. You might be asked to answer phones, stuff envelopes, or distribute leaflets. On Election Day you'll feel a surge of pride knowing you went out and tried to effect change, even if your candidate doesn't win—this time.

AT THE POLLS

Even if you're not old enough to vote yet, you might be able to serve as a poll worker on election day. This involves helping voters sign in, answering any questions they have about how to cast their ballot, and helping to secure the ballots for counting after the polls close. Check with your local department of elections for details on the minimum age. You might even get paid for your efforts.

72 Feed Those in Need

If you've ever missed breakfast because you woke up late and had to rush to school, or if you've had to wait for your takeout longer than you expected, you may have moaned that you were "starving." But for many people, hunger is a much more serious situation than one missed or delayed meal. But more than forty-seven million Americans, including one in five children, face hunger regularly. Their families can't afford enough food or can't access food in their price range.

Most towns and cities have programs for feeding the hungry. There's likely at least one religious institution or nonprofit organizations working tirelessly to get food to those who need it. Those groups generally welcome volunteers.

How to Do It

Research your options. Find out which groups are active in your community. There are probably more than you're aware of, as these orgs don't usually have enough money to do major advertising. They all run their operations—and their volunteer programs—a little differently. Decide if you'd like to work with a certain demographic: homeless families with small children, housebound senior citizens, teenage runaways. Once you find a place you like, fill out an online application or talk to the program organizer about volunteer opportunities, schedule, and training requirements.

Pitch in. Try to commit to volunteering on a regular schedule, even if it's only a few hours a month. Treat your volunteer work as if it were a paying job. Your boss may not be able to fire you if you skip work, but if you don't show up, you'll be letting folks down.

Donate. If you're unable to find time in your busy schedule for volunteering, these organizations usually take monetary donations. They might also occasionally run community food drives. They'll provide a list of foods they're collecting. Stick to the items that are requested. And buy them from a grocery store—don't use a food drive as an excuse to clear expired or otherwise unwanted items out of your cupboards. Remember that the people you're feeding deserve the dignity of high-quality food.

BEYOND CHRISTMAS

Soup kitchens and other food-delivery programs always get a surge of volunteers around the holidays. It's natural for people to try to help during this season, but your services are much more valuable during the rest of the year.

73 Understand How a Farm Works

Most Americans today are pretty clueless about where their food comes from. Farmers only make up around 2 percent of the US population, but they play the crucial role of feeding the other 98 percent of us. Visiting a farm will help you understand more about the food you eat, the labor that goes into food production, and why treating natural resources with respect is essential. Rural dwellers probably already know a thing or two about how much work it takes to get eggs from the henhouse to the table, but for those who think their breakfast is grown in the back rooms of the supermarket, a taste of farm life is a valuable experience.

How to Do It

Find a farm. There's bound to be at least a few acres of farmland within a few hours' drive or bus ride. Contact the farm in advance to see if you can book a tour.

Get hands-on. Many small commercial farms offer day trip programs featuring all sorts of interactive opportunities, from plowing fields with oxen and picking veggies to milking cows and churning butter. Don't be afraid to ask questions during a tour or activity.

Reflect. Think about what new skills you can bring back to your ordinary life. What insights can you employ in tending to your own garden? What changes can you make to lessen your environmental impact? (The meat industry is responsible for *a lot* of greenhouse emissions.) Think about your place in the complex system of getting food from the earth to your plate.

A GROWING CONCERN

Many farmers have taken an interest in sustainable agriculture—efforts to grow food without harming the environment. This means no chemical dumps or significant disruption to the local ecosystem. And sustainable practices aren't just for farmers. You too can lessen your ecological footprint by cutting down on your shopping, driving less, and switching to reusable products.

74 Write a Letter to the Editor

Do you have strong opinions about what's going on in your community? Want to express your impassioned beliefs beyond the dinner table and cafeteria? Reach out to a wide readership by submitting a letter to the editor of your local newspaper. Most papers devote a page or two of each edition to these short essays written by community members. Maybe you've thought of a great reason why that abandoned lot should be turned into a skate park. Maybe you want your city to host an architectural competition for a monument to victims of a disaster. Or maybe you want to speak out about your views on a topic of broader importance, like an overseas conflict or attacks on the freedom to read. The more specific your letter, the better. The point is to bring people's attention to important issues and spark public dialogue.

How to Do It

Find a paper. If you don't have a local newspaper, find the nearest city-based or regional publication. Check the website for a submission portal or check the paper itself for submission guidelines. There may be a word-count limit—usually around a couple hundred words—or content restrictions to keep in mind.

Write your piece. Catch readers' attention with a snappy subject line and get to the point quickly. Lead with the most important information. State your position clearly. Emphasize why this issue matters. Mention verified facts and statistics. Appeal to people's reason as well as their emotions.

Keep trying. Not every letter to the editor submitted to a paper is published. If yours isn't chosen, you can still get your opinion out there by posting it online. And you can submit another letter in the future.

SAY IT IN A DRAWING

You can also submit cartoons to your local paper. If writing isn't your thing, express your views in pictures. A single-panel cartoon with a pithy caption is worth the proverbial thousand words.

75 Donate to a Homeless Shelter

Homelessness is a crisis in America, affecting hundreds of thousands of people. You probably know at least one person who's a single health crisis, job loss, or natural disaster away from becoming unhoused. Most of us *are* that person. It's shockingly easy to lose the roof over your head, along with the possessions that made it home. Yet in many areas, resources for unhoused people are scarce.

Such a big problem can feel overwhelming, but there are ways you can help. You can start by collecting items to make a much-needed donation to a local homeless shelter.

How to Do It

Cull your closets. Have family members set aside clothing in good condition that no longer fits or hasn't been worn in ages. Coats and sweaters are particularly useful in cold climates.

Gather necessities. Set aside unopened and unused (and unexpired!) household items that clear the "like new" bar, or organize a fundraiser to buy new items. Backpacks and sleeping bags are extremely useful for unhoused people, as are blankets and pillows. Other items in high demand include shampoo, toothpaste, medical supplies like bandages and first-aid kits, batteries, diapers, toys, and paperback books.

Pack up and deliver. Put items in boxes and contact a local shelter to arrange for delivery. Some organizations will pick up boxes from your home—but don't expect them to take ratty old furniture or torn mittens off your hands. They can only use items in good shape. Save the organizations some time by separating the good stuff from the junk and throwing out the junk (or recycling it, when possible) yourself.

NEW GIFT INSTEAD OF THRIFT

Instead of donating your holey old socks, buy some inexpensive socks, underwear, or other personal items and donate them while they're brand new. The people who receive them will appreciate the feeling of wearing something straight out of the box.

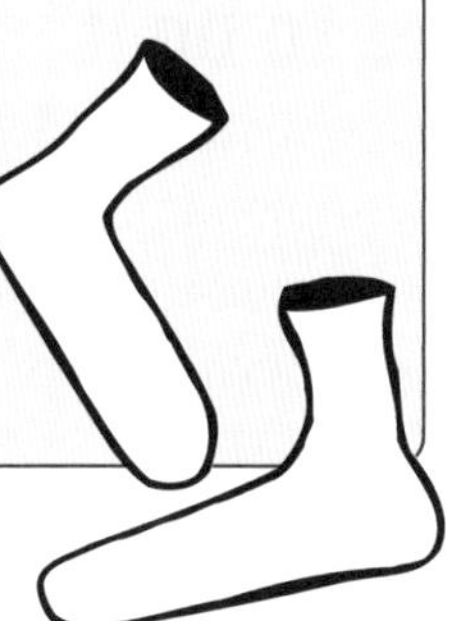

76 Raise Money for a Charity

Helping out in your community is often about sweat equity—meaning that your volunteer time, friendliness, enthusiasm, and donation of resources are just as important as cash contributions. Sometimes, though, it takes dollars—and lots of them—to assist those in need. Raising money for a charity or cause takes persistence and persuasiveness, but your passion can convince fellow philanthropists and cheapskate skeptics alike to fork over a little cash.

How to Do It

Choose a cause. Identify a charity whose mission moves you. Maybe you know someone with diabetes, cancer, or another illness that requires research and preventive care outreach. Maybe a natural disaster has wreaked havoc on a city, or a local family is being targeted by immigration legislation.

Set goals. Work with a representative from the organization to raise funds. Decide on a target amount that's realistic but substantial. Recruit allies to help you organize

Choose a method. You could host a car wash or a bake sale. If you're connected to your local music scene, organize a concert or an open mic night, charging a cover or accepting donations at the door.

Promote. Publicize your event with social media posts, digital and physical flyers, and information sheets. Make sure people know that even if they can't make it, they can still donate to the charity directly. Afterward, count the cash and deliver all proceeds to the charity. Every dollar makes a difference.

Don't reinvent the wheel. There might already be a robust fundraiser connected to the issue you care about. If you'd rather join an existing effort than create your own, that's great too! For instance, you might participate in a walk, bike, or run for your cause. Solicit donations from friends and family. Spread the word through social media.

CROWDFUNDING CONUNDRUM

Crowdfunding platforms like GoFundMe are a popular way for individuals to raise money for medical emergencies, disaster relief, and other debilitating expenses. It's great to contribute to these efforts. Just remember that it's equally important to donate to organizations that fight the root causes of these problems, so that people won't always *need* to turn to crowdfunding in emergency situations.

77 Get a Job

You might already be all over this. Lots of kids start working early, whether at a family business or local business. But if you've been cruising through high school without any employment experience under your belt, you're missing out. Yes, you're already busy enough with schoolwork, football practice, and playing Fortnite—but if you can spare just a little time each week for a job, it'll pay dividends in the future. Even if you don't *need* the money, who couldn't do with a little extra weight in their wallet when walking around the mall or taking a crush on a date?

Employment also has benefits beyond the paycheck. It gives you confidence, independence from your parents, and a competitive edge in college applications. It also gives you something to put on your résumé when you really do need to start looking for a job.

How to Do It

Scout opportunities. If your school has career advisers, they may keep a list of job opportunities to look into. Keep an eye out for "help wanted" or "now hiring" signs in the windows of businesses. Search for "part-time jobs near me" online. You can talk to someone at the business about handing in an application, but they'll likely point you toward an online listing anyway.

Apply. You'll need to fill out the application with contact info, employment history (if you have any), and a résumé (if you have one). Don't stress too

ADVENTURES IN BABYSITTING

A paid babysitting gig is a great way to earn money without committing to a "regular" job. Dirty diapers are a drag, but the vocation has its perks, especially if you enjoy being around kids. Start by babysitting for a close relative who'll be forgiving of minor mistakes. Figure out what age range you're comfortable being responsible for and what hourly rate seems fair. Then spread the word through social media and your friend network as you seek out more clients.

much if you don't have anything to put down for these sections. Entry-level positions are often designed for new workers.

Add references. Select a few responsible adults who aren't relatives and who can vouch for your reliability and skill. Previous employers, teachers, and coaches are good options. Check with any potential references in advance to confirm they're willing to speak to prospective employers. Include each person's name, their relationship to you, and their contact info with your application.

Persist. Send applications to multiple employers, as you're unlikely to hear back from many places. Getting ghosted for a job is a bummer, but it's common and not personal. If you *really* want a certain position but haven't heard back, try contacting the employer directly. They might appreciate your enthusiasm and invite you in for an interview.

78 Write a Résumé

Some after-school jobs are easy to come by. A neighbor asks you to babysit or your dad's friend hires you to help at his shop. But unless you're ridiculously lucky, you won't get every job based on connections alone. To stand a fighting chance in a competitive labor market, you'll need a résumé.

This one-page summary of your specialized skills, knowledge, and experience makes the case that you're a perfect candidate for the record shop down the street. It provides your prospective employer with information about your experience. And it sends the message that you're organized, ambitious, and serious about working for them. Sending in a killer résumé along with your application will greatly boost your odds of landing your dream job (or at least the best job available). Résumés are also essential for internships, scholarships, and even certain volunteer positions. Mastering the delicate art of résumé-making will help you secure bigger opportunities down the road.

How to Do It

Look at other résumés. Study examples online, or ask to see an older sibling's or friend's most recent one. They might even offer you a few pointers. An English teacher or school adviser can also point you in the right direction.

Fill in the blanks. You can either start with a blank Word doc or import a free template. At the top, list your contact info, including your full name, phone number, and personal email address. Next, consider including a one-sentence objective. This isn't absolutely necessary, but it can help fill space if your résumé is running short. Here's an example: "To contribute my shopping expertise and enthusiasm to the retail sector." Below that, list all your previous work experience in reverse-chronological order. Under each job title, include a bullet-pointed list of your duties.

Get creative. If you have no work experience, that's okay. You can fill out this section with extracurricular activities, especially anything involving a leadership position, like captain of the debate team or treasurer of the key club. Then add any special skills you possess. These should directly relate to the field you're applying to work in: coding for a computer-based job, fluency in a second language and strong interpersonal skills for retail.

Proofread. Make sure your résumé is cleanly formatted, is easy to read, and fits nicely on one page. Have an adult look over it for any mistakes.

COVER LETTERS

Some positions require you to submit a cover letter along with your résumé. This is a brief, three-to-four-paragraph essay that expresses your enthusiasm and explains why you would be the perfect candidate for the job.

Keep it handy. Don't delete your résumé once you land a job. Save a copy of it around for your next job search and add to it as your life and work experience grows.

79 Make and Follow a Budget

If you have a job—or very generous parents—you have some money coming in. Even if you're forced to use some of it on necessities, you may have at least a little left over to spend on yourself. Rather than blow it *all* on video game microtransactions or a pair of expensive sneakers, you can divide your cash into categories; keep track of how, when, and where you spend; and set limits on certain types of spending. Welcome to making a budget!

It's not the most exciting thing in the world, but it can teach you a lot about yourself and your habits. It'll help you visualize the difference between financial needs, like transportation costs and school supplies, and financial desires, like takeout and extra clothes. Ultimately, it can help you be smarter and more strategic about how you spend money.

How to Do It

Make a spreadsheet. Either on paper or in a digital spreadsheet, list everything you spend money on throughout a typical month. Separate your table into categories: clothes, movie tickets, eating out, online subscriptions, etc. If you have your own bank account and debit card, go through previous statements and input the exact amounts from the charges on your card. If not, you'll need to manually track your spending for at least a week.

Total it up. After you're done collecting data, add up how much you spend in each category over a certain period. Compare the numbers. Maybe you're spending a lot on clothes. Did you spend more on gas than usual last month, and do you know why?

Calculate your max. You may have access to a set amount of money each month—from a job, an allowance, or a combination. Or your cash flow may fluctuate depending on how many lawns you mowed or how generous your grandma is feeling. Figure out the total amount you can count on and whether you've got anything left over at the end of a typical month.

Make a plan. Adjust your spending to better reflect your needs and financial limitations. Try to spend less than your total monthly max. Reasonable spending and saving habits will make the occasional splurge more manageable.

CHOOSE NOT TO CHARGE

Credit card companies specifically target teens through advertising, knowing that people in your age group are tempted by the promise of a no-holds-barred shopping spree. Don't let them get you! It's easy to "charge it" now, but big balances and interest pile up fast and can be hard to pay off later. If you're not careful, you can get yourself into a financial mess. Use a debit card or cash instead.

80 Open a Savings Account

You're certainly entitled to spend your money however you want. But it's never too early to start saving—for college tuition, a car, or another big purchase. Having a reserve of cash can be extremely useful when you're a little older and bills start piling up. Plus you'll have extra peace of mind knowing that you can cover emergency expenses. If you've got nothing stowed away so far, it's time to open a bank account and start saving.

How to Do It

Head to the bank. If you're under eighteen, you might need a parent or guardian to come along for a few signatures, but the process should be largely painless. Many banks offer special deals for teens who are opening their first account, so ask the bank's representative to explain the options.

Consider a high-interest option. The interest rate is the percent by which your money will increase every year without your having to lift a finger. The money just has to sit in the account, and it'll automatically start incurring interest. Most interest rates on savings accounts are super low, but if you manage to save up a larger chunk of cash that you're confident you won't need right away, you can put it in a certificate of deposit (CD), which offers a much higher interest rate as long as you don't withdraw any money for a set period of time—say, a year or eighteen months.

Keep track. Download your bank's app or regularly check their website to keep track of your savings. If you've got a checking account with the same bank, you can instantly move money between the accounts. So if a paycheck comes in, you can siphon off part of it into your savings. Or if a surprise expense comes up, you can move some money from savings to checking and pay that bill.

A LITTLE BIT HELPS

Try to put away at least twenty dollars every month. That's just one less night of takeout each month. You'd be surprised at how quickly these small contributions can add up.

81 Understand the Stock Market

Buy low. Sell high. Diversify your portfolio by dumping those risky hedge funds and opting instead for a blue-chip mutual fund.

Huh?

Stock market terminology and financial data are like a foreign language. You have to study and practice it to understand it. But with time and dedication, you can learn the lingo and the rules of the game.

The stock market, which has a long history in the US and an even longer one abroad, is perhaps the world's biggest casino. To play the market, people buy investments, such as stocks, which are actually small portions of a company. If the company does well during the year, investors generally make money. If that company does poorly (or worse, goes out of business), investors can be in trouble. Experienced investors—or at least

CRYPTOCURRENCY

At first glance, the cryptocurrency market can look a lot like the stock market, with different coins constantly fluctuating in value. But these coins are decentralized, entirely digital pieces of currency. Their value isn't tied to the performance of a physical company. And since it's relatively new technology, the crypto market is largely unregulated, which means it's rife with scams and risk.

the investment firms they pay to manage their money—try to gauge when to buy stock and when to sell it to maximize profits and minimize losses. But the market is unpredictable, and even the most skillful "gamblers" sometimes lose. It's not a game to be played lightly.

You have to be eighteen to participate in the stock market, but you can start learning about it anytime.

How to Do It

Follow the money. Pick a few stocks to follow and chart their ups and downs over a period of three to six months. This information is easy to find online: "[company] stock price" will do the trick. Pick companies whose missions you admire, or ones you want to learn about, and track their stocks' progress on a spreadsheet.

Follow the news. To better understand why the stocks fluctuate, check the latest news on the companies. Maybe they announce a merger or roll out a new product. See how recent developments affect their stock prices. You can also check out articles in the *Wall Street Journal*, *Fortune*, and CNBC for more in-depth coverage.

Follow your instincts. At some point, when you have a few hundred or thousand to spare, understanding your investment options will save you from going broke. By the time you're able to legally participate in the game, you'll have a basic idea of how to play. The most important guiding principle: never invest money that you cannot live without.

82 Take Care of a Pet

When it comes to companionship, reliability, and emotional support, animals offer distinct advantages over humans: They listen attentively to your rants, they stick to a predictable routine of eating, sleeping, playing, and pooping, and they provide unconditional love as long as you scratch their bellies and reward their obedience with ample treats.

Taking care of a pet is a great way to learn how to be responsible for another living creature, and your very own cat, dog, mouse, lizard, fish, or eight-foot boa constrictor will teach you life lessons about the importance of dependability and loyalty. Just be sure you're ready for the commitment before heading to the adoption center. The well-being of a living, breathing creature is a big responsibility that shouldn't be taken on lightly.

How to Do It

Plan carefully. Consider the size of your living space and your amount of available time. Dogs take up a lot of room, are very hands-on, and need plenty of exercise, while cats are more independent and like to pretend they don't really need you once they've outgrown the ball-of-string phase. Think about costs too. A hamster or goldfish won't set you back nearly as much as a purebred golden retriever puppy.

Adopt ethically. Never buy a pet from an unlicensed breeder. Responsible, humane breeders are upfront about their practices and costs. And those costs can be substantial! Consider adopting a pet from an animal rescue organization or an animal shelter. Shelters are bursting with animals who deserve forever homes—and they charge much less than specialty breeders.

Meet and greet. Scan animals' profiles on shelter websites and make an appointment to meet a few animals. It's important to get a sense of an animal's personality and specific needs before taking it home. Get your new pet microchipped, spayed or neutered, and checked out by a vet. (Responsible shelters offer or facilitate these services as part of the adoption fee.)

Train 'em up. Whether you adopt a floppy-eared puppy, cuddly feline, or bashful turtle with intimacy issues, your pet will have a distinct personality that you'll need to nurture or modify with training. Read up on training techniques or find a pro trainer if needed.

TIME MANAGEMENT

Most pets need to be fed on a certain schedule. Many need to have their habitats cleaned regularly or at least need you to get rid of their poop. (This includes dogs—when you go for a walk, always bring along plastic baggies for scooping and easy disposal.) Some need grooming, such as nail-trimming, brushing, and the occasional bath for dogs. Some need medicines at specific times, especially as they age. Most need regular check-ups at the vet. If you're struggling with the time commitment of keeping a pet, approach a family member to ask for backup.

83 Nurture a Houseplant

Do you want to take care of a living thing . . . but not one that barks all night, empties its bladder unexpectedly, and chews through your mom's curtains? A friendly houseplant will spruce up your space with color and ambiance. By taking in carbon dioxide and giving off oxygen, indoor plants clean your environment while lending character to your desktops and nightstands. You can even name your plant and develop a relationship with it. It will be exciting to see your foliaceous friend grow and thrive under your care.

How to Do It

Pick a plant. Ficus trees, lithops, begonias, African violets, coleus, pothos, ferns, parlor maples, and bamboo all tend to grow well indoors, and you don't need much expertise to keep them healthy and happy. Plants from the succulent family, including the soothing cure-all aloe vera, are a breeze to nurture (they don't need much water). Intensely colored bromeliads require just the right amount of water and light but are well worth the effort—they'll transform your bedroom into a tropical paradise.

Know your plant's needs. Consult a worker at the garden store or do some research online to find out the right type of potting soil for your plant. Find out how much light and water it needs. Set reminders on your calendar or phone so you can stick to the right watering schedule. Underwatering and overwatering are the chief causes of premature demise.

CONVERSATIONS WITH YOUR CACTUS?

In his 1848 book *Nanna, or About the Soul-Life of Plants*, German physicist and philosopher Gustav Theodor Fechner promoted the idea of talking to plants to aid their growth, believing that greenery responds to emotion. While this theory has never been proved, there's a certain therapeutic quality in yapping to your succulent about this week's math test.

84 Look into Talk Therapy

Maybe you've always thought of yourself as someone who doesn't "need" therapy. Or maybe you've wished for a therapist but assumed your family can't afford one. But don't let assumptions hold you back. As you prepare to launch into adulthood, it's useful to have an understanding of what talk therapy can offer and a sense of how to find good care.

How to Do It

Know what it is. Psychotherapy, or talk therapy, is the practice of speaking with a mental health professional to process emotions, adjust behavior, and generally improve or maintain mental health. A typical therapy session lasts about an hour. Most therapists offer flexibility in how often you can schedule sessions: weekly, every other week, once a month, or even twice a week. Some people who use talk therapy also use medication. Talk therapists typically can't prescribe medications, but they can recommend medication options for you to discuss with your family doctor or a specialist.

Know what it's for. Therapy isn't only for people who are struggling—though it can certainly help someone through a short-term or ongoing crisis. Even if every aspect of your life is going swimmingly (what's your secret?!), therapy sessions can be chances for self-reflection and self-improvement.

Know the costs. Therapy is often expensive if you don't have insurance or can't find a provider who accepts your insurance. But some therapists offer tiered cost options geared toward their patients' financial situations.

Know how to find it. Qualified therapists may have months-long waiting lists for new patients. It can be worthwhile to get on the waiting lists for a few therapists in your area. Some therapists offer remote appointments so you don't have to get to a physical office.

Know how to use it. You might need to try a few therapists before you find the right fit. This can be frustrating, time consuming, and more expensive than it should be. But you shouldn't be afraid to leave a therapist you're not clicking with. A good therapist will listen carefully, give you space to sift through your thoughts, and share honest impressions without jumping to conclusions. A therapist you're comfortable with and who can offer you the kind of support you need is worth the wait.

TAKE IT OFFLINE

Online counseling platforms can seem attractive: They're cheap or free; therapists are supposedly always on call; and you can connect with someone through your phone without having to leave the couch. But these programs are often understaffed, questionably secure, or downright shady. You'll likely be better off holding out for a therapist with an established practice. (If you find yourself in an acute crisis and need immediate support, the 988 hotline operates 24/7.)

85 Get a Driver's License

You've suffered through years of having to be shuttled around by a parent or older sibling anytime you want to travel farther than the gas station around the corner. You're probably more than ready to get behind the wheel yourself and experience the freedoms that automotive transportation can grant you. Getting your driver's license is a teenage rite of passage in the parts of the country that lack ample public transportation (which is most of them). Suddenly, your world expands beyond the distances you can reach on foot or bike, even if you won't be hitting the road on a cross-continental road trip just yet.

But driving comes with its own responsibilities. When you're behind the wheel, you're responsible for the lives of everyone in the car and on the road near you. If you follow the rules of the road and don't abuse the privilege, driving can be an important step toward adulthood.

How to Do It

Study. Rules and regulations differ from state to state, but in general, it's best to start by taking a driver's education course, either at school or at a private training center. Search online for the offerings near you. Once you graduate from this course and pass a written test, you'll be rewarded with your learner's permit. This small identification card lets you legally get behind the wheel, as long as there's a fully licensed adult in the passenger seat.

Drive. You'll probably be required to take driving lessons with an approved trainer. While learning, it's best to start in a big, empty parking lot, gradually working up to streets and, when you're ready, multilane highways.

Take the test. When you take your driver's test at the DMV, don't be bummed out if you fail the first or second time. That's very common. This is one test you absolutely want to ace, so keep studying and practicing until you're completely comfortable changing lanes, checking your mirrors and—worst of them all—parallel parking.

PUT THE PHONE DOWN

You've probably had "Don't text and drive" drilled into your mind since birth, but it can't be overstated. Car accidents are terrible and traumatizing, even when they're minor—and they often aren't. Don't jeopardize your safety and the safety of others by picking up your phone while on the road.

86 Learn Basic Car Maintenance

Whether you've recently gotten your license or prefer to ride shotgun while a friend does the driving so you can have aux, it's crucial to learn the basics of car maintenance. Changing a tire isn't as tough as it looks, and checking tire pressure, oil, windshield wiper fluid, and brake fluid levels are as easy as pumping gas. You don't have to be a full-on mechanic, but a knowledge of the basics will help you keep a car in better shape and save you tons of money in repair costs. Being prepared on the road also instills confidence and independence, since you won't have to call your dad from the side of the highway again.

How to Do It

Find an expert. Ask a friend or family member who knows something about cars to give you a crash course on what's happening under the hood. It's best to go to someone who can teach you what to do without being condescending. If that sounds impossible, look up basic car maintenance tutorials online.

Ask questions. Have your tutor explain how the engine gets going when you turn the key in the ignition and tap the gas pedal. Get tips on how to check the oil and other fluids (some should be checked after the engine has warmed up, while others—such as the oil—should be checked when the engine is cool). Learn how to fill up a tire and jump-start a battery with cables.

Be prepared. Outfit the trunk with a spare tire, a tire jack, a quart or two of oil, a gas can, jumper cables, and emergency flares. Don't forget a rag to wipe the oil dipstick and a tire gauge to check the pressure. Know roughly how often your oil needs to be changed and take it into the shop once you're nearing that threshold.

UNDER THE HOOD

Here are some basic car parts you'll want to be able to identify.

- battery: a big black box with two knobs—often red and black—protruding from the top
- engine: usually the biggest hunk of metal under the hood
- engine coolant, usually an atomic green liquid
- oil tank: a reservoir with a dipstick, usually marked "oil" (but be careful—some cars have a separate dipstick to check transmission fluid)
- main fuse relay box: a black box under the hood that's usually marked

87 Assemble a Toolbox

Whether you're already a pro or completely clueless when it comes to household repairs, it's a good idea to outfit a toolbox with a dozen or so essential items and learn how to use them. Instead of having to rely on someone else to fix stuff, you can get things done when and how you want them—and prepare for times when you're on your own.

How to Do It

Gather tools. Head to a hardware store (or their online store page) to stock up on essentials. Do some research on brands and types ahead of time. If you find yourself choosing between two identical-looking wrenches, you can ask an employee for a recommendation. You might also find tools in good condition at a garage sale, a thrift store, or a relative's basement.

Tackle tasks. These tools should get you started on simple projects like hanging a picture frame, cutting speaker wire, and assembling Ikea-type furniture.

Build the toolbox. Your skills will advance and your needs will shift. Add specialty tools as needed. If you have enough cash, pay a bit more for better-quality tools. They'll last for decades.

Treat tools well. Keep tools clean and dry because dirt and water will rust them. Machine oil is an effective cleaner, and steel wool will polish them like new. Add a can of WD-40 to your kit and give all the tools a thorough going-over every few times you use them.

TOOLS OF YOUR TRADE

Here are some tools that come in handy for a wide variety of projects:

- hammer
- pliers
- wrench
- large and small screwdrivers (both flat and Phillips screwdrivers)
- cordless drill with a set of bits
- utility knife
- level
- assorted nails and screws
- tape measure
- gloves
- safety goggles
- flashlight

88 Learn Basic Clothes Maintenance

You might already wash, fold, and mend your own clothes. If so, pat yourself on your fresh-smelling back. If not, it's time to discover what happens between when they get tossed into the hamper and when they land freshly cleaned and neatly folded on your bed. Gather your faded jeans, favorite hoodie, and funky socks, and get the spin cycle going. While you're at it, learn some other aspects of basic clothes maintenance: ironing, sewing buttons, and hemming pants or skirts.

Doing your own laundry comes with more benefits than just parental approval. It prevents other people from shrinking your favorite T-shirt down to Barbie doll size, going through your pockets, or mistakenly bleaching your dark blue denims until they're no longer dark . . . or blue.

How to Do It

Sort. Every washing machine has various settings related to clothing type. You may have to do a couple of separate loads. Delicate items such as lingerie should be washed separately on a delicate cycle—or even by hand in the sink. Separating lights and darks is also a common practice. Some people wash light-colored clothes in warm or hot water, which is best for getting out gross stains, and wash darks in cold, so they won't fade or run. When in doubt, cold water usually gets the job done (and saves energy), as long as you use a good detergent.

Prep. Use a liquid detergent or detergent pod. Check your washing machine to see if there's a special place you should put it or if you can just pour it into the basin. If you spilled salad dressing on your jeans or cut yourself shaving and got blood on your collar, use a gentle stain remover. These come in a few different forms, including a special powder you put in the washer before starting it and a liquid you place directly on the stain; follow the directions on the package.

Dry. Check tags to see if clothing can be tumble-dried. If you don't want certain clothing items to fade or shrink, you're better off hang drying them than tossing them in the dryer. Some delicate items should be laid flat to dry. Fold your clothes as soon as they're done drying to avoid wrinkles.

And beyond. For mending, ironing, and sewing advice, ask your resident laundry expert or check out online tutorials. Knowing how to mend clothes will not only save you money but allow you to hold onto sentimental pieces long after they're past their prime.

STEAM PRESS ON THE GO

Don't have time to iron? Take your wrinkled clothes with you into the bathroom when you shower. Hang them on the back of the door or lay them on a flat surface. Then shower with the door closed. The hot steam produced from the shower will take the wrinkles (at least most of them) out of your clothes.

89 Learn CPR

The heart is a resilient muscle, but sometimes resilience isn't enough. When someone's heart stops, it's often fatal. But if you act quickly, you can help. It's possible to save a person who's undergoing cardiac arrest (the medical term for a heart attack) by performing cardiopulmonary resuscitation, also known as CPR. This a fairly easy skill to learn—one that could save a life someday.

How to Do It

Sign up. CPR training is available for free at professional, volunteer, and government organizations in nearly every city. You can also pay to take a course. Search online to find classes in your area.

Show up. A basic CPR course should only take between two and four hours. You'll learn how to quickly assess a victim's condition and apply lifesaving procedures: consist of mouth-to-mouth resuscitation (breathing air into the victim's lungs) and chest compressions. The point of mouth-to-mouth is to keep oxygen flowing into the blood via the lungs. Chest compressions keep the blood flowing, especially to the brain.

Get help. CPR is only a first step. It buys some time until a medical professional arrives to restore the victim's heartbeat, usually with an automated external defibrillator. So it's absolutely essential for someone on the scene to call 911 as soon as the incident occurs. Then do CPR while you wait for help to arrive. If there's another bystander, they may be able to tag-team with you so that you don't wear yourself out doing chest compressions.

MAKE A SPLASH

CPR can also be used to save the life of a drowning victim, once they're out of the water. If you've mastered CPR and are an experienced swimmer, consider becoming a lifeguard. The American Red Cross and local safety organizations train lifeguards. You must be at least fifteen years old and devote twenty to forty hours to learning rescue skills to become a certified lifeguard. Certification lasts two years. You'll help people stay safe, hang out at the beach or pool, *and* get paid for your efforts.

90 Be Prepared for an Emergency

From earthquakes to hurricanes to tornadoes, nature loves to humble us with mega disasters that devastate communities and change people's lives. And climate change increases the likelihood and severity of these events in certain parts of the world. It's impossible to predict if and when you might be caught in a natural catastrophe, but you might lessen the impact by being prepared. Rather than stress out about the unknown, take an afternoon to organize essential provisions and learn some simple procedures. Then do your best to let go of the worry. You'll be as prepared as you can be.

How to Do It

Go over household basics. Gather with your family and make sure everyone knows how to turn off the gas, switch on circuit breakers, and change fuses.

Consolidate supplies. Store extra fuses in a utility drawer or cabinet, along with light bulbs, flashlights, batteries, candles, and matches.

Have emergency contacts. Make sure everyone has numbers for family members and family doctors saved in their phones. Know the location of the nearest emergency room—you might need to take a loved one there for treatment.

Maintain a first-aid kit. You can buy a kit or put one together with drugstore purchases. Include bandages, antibiotic ointment, aspirin, bottled water, and medications taken by anyone in the family. Keep the first-aid kit with your emergency supplies.

Stock up. Keep a supply of bottled water on hand in case the tap water supply is tainted, and gradually build up a reserve of nonperishable food that doesn't have to be heated (pineapple chunks, peanut butter, baked beans). With the help of a sturdy can opener, you'll have plenty to eat if cooking isn't possible. Don't forget food for your pets.

Pack a bag. Assemble a "grab and go" backpack or duffel bag that includes extra clothes, some food (granola bars and dried fruit are good options), spare chargers, and copies of important documents. Keep it in a spot where you can easily grab it if you need to evacuate quickly.

CELL PHONE LIFESAVER

Many smartphones allow you to store a unique medical ID, which is accessible from your home screen even without a passcode. Take a few minutes to input your name, date of birth, and any medical conditions or allergies you have. That way, paramedics can access this crucial information even if you're incapacitated.

91 Try a New Hairstyle

Have you been rocking the same hairdo since kindergarten graduation? It might be time to leave your comfort zone and experiment with some new follicular fashion. Your hair can reflect some aspect of your personality and identity. A cut, style, or dye job is one way to express your ever-evolving self. And if your experiment isn't a success, well, hair grows back.

How to Do It

Know your hair type. Thin or thick? Dry or oily? Straight, wavy, curled? Prone to frizz? Prone to going flat? The more you know about your hair and its specific needs, the more easily you can choose products and styles that'll help it look its best.

Pick a cut. Search social media for a style that speaks to you. Celebrities and influencers are constantly showing off new looks. Study what works well on them and adapt their expensive designer looks for something that fits your budget. Discuss options with your barber or stylist.

APPRECIATE, DON'T APPROPRIATE

Some hairstyles and hair practices are rooted in specific cultures. If you admire a stunning look but aren't a member of the culture it's connected to, it's best not to try copying it on your own head. You can respect this boundary and still have nearly limitless cut, style, and accessory options to choose from.

Shift the vibe. You might decide to get a familiar cut but *wear* it completely differently than you ever have before. Or you might use hair dye or colored conditioner to radiate a new vibe. (Do plenty of research on the best and safest products, lest that dollar store box dye leave your hair fried for months.) Even trying a new conditioner or mousse can be surprisingly transformative.

Rinse and repeat. In a few months, change it up again!

92 Confess a Crush

You've been staring at your latest love from across the school cafeteria for weeks or even months, trying to work up the nerve to make your move. When they walk by, your stomach flip-flops and you start to sweat. A moment later, you're kicking yourself for not trying to squeak out a simple hi.

Crushes are like too much candy—they make you feel hyper and giddy and then sort of sick and exhausted from the sugar crash. The best way to get over these symptoms is with a confession. You'll never know how they feel until you declare your undying love (or temporary like). So muster every ounce of self-esteem you've got and get ready to approach the object of your affection.

How to Do It

Don't overthink it. You can spend the rest of your life workshopping the perfect opening line, which you'll most likely blow anyway, or you can just take the plunge to get past those first few awkward moments. If your crush is a complete stranger, break the ice with a brief intro—your name and something about where you've seen each other before, maybe in a class or on the basketball court. Chat about school or mutual friends for a bit.

Take a hint. If you get the cold shoulder, back off. You can try again another time if their attitude seems friendlier, but don't keep pushing if they act annoyed, bored, or uncomfortable. If you get smiles and some flirting back, that's your cue to bring up a date.

Cut to the chase. Keep the suggestion light. You're testing the waters, not proposing marriage. If your crush is someone you know well, like a close friend or a teammate, you can indicate your deeper feelings in a lowkey way: "I've been wondering if you'd like to get ice cream one-on-one sometime." "I know we've known each other since third grade so this might seem a little weird, but how would you feel about going to the dance together?" If you've got less history with your crush, ask if you can have their number or suggest meeting up at this weekend's game or concert.

Roll with the response. If you face rejection, take it on the chin. It might sting for a while, but in the long run, you'll be glad you got a straight answer rather than a lifetime of what-ifs. If you get a "maybe," that could be a potential yes or a polite no. If you're genuinely not sure, feel free to ask, and make it clear you'll respect a no. If it's a yes, start planning your date!

SLIDING INTO THEIR DMS

It can be tempting to ask out your crush over text. That way, you could avoid the awkwardness of in-person confession (and possible rejection). While this method may work sometimes, it's better to do it in person. Your crush will be impressed by your confidence and flattered that you cared enough to ask them out face-to-face. It's also much easier to gauge their emotional reaction if you can see their facial expression, hear their tone, and feel their vibe.

93 Tell Someone Your Darkest Secret

Have you done something that's keeping you awake at night from embarrassment, shame, or fear? Is there a skeleton in your closet whose rattling bones remind you of a one-time mistake or ongoing mess? While many personal activities can and should remain private—revealed only to the pages of your diary—some deeds deserve to be shared with a confidant. Whether you have a crush on your best friend's girlfriend, shoplifted some makeup, or cheated on your history final, unburden your conscience by confessing your deepest, darkest secret.

How to Do It

Call in backup. If you've done something seriously illegal, are participating in an activity that's dangerous to you or others (like abusing drugs or alcohol), or have witnessed or experienced serious harm, talk to your parents, your guidance counselor, or another trusted adult before the situation gets any further out of control.

Spill the tea. If your secret isn't jeopardizing anyone's health or landing you on the FBI's Most Wanted list, sharing your secret with a close friend or sibling can be cathartic. Your confidant should be someone you trust not to blab about it to everyone they know.

Move forward. Once the words are out of your mouth, you'll most likely feel a strong sense of relief. Discuss the situation with your confidant and calmly decide what, if anything, you need to do next.

ONLINE AND ANONYMOUS

If you want to confess your secret but can't bring yourself to tell anyone face-to-face, you can post it to an online forum or anonymous social media page that can't be traced back to you. You might even receive advice from a few digital Good Samaritans. Just remember that not everyone online is an expert! Take the feedback that feels genuinely supportive and helpful; leave the rest in the downvoted comments.

94 Get a Piercing

Piercings aren't for everybody, but septum rings snakebites might sound right up your alley. You might've gotten your ears pierced at Claire's when you were four years old, but the wonderful world of piercings doesn't start and end at a shopping mall. Piercings can be a mode of self-expression. And they're much less permanent than a face tat, which will probably need to wait until you're older.

How to Do It

Get the green light. If you're under eighteen, you'll probably need parental or guardian consent. Make sure the signee knows that this isn't a spur-of-the-moment idea but is something you've carefully considered. Remind them that a piercing isn't usually permanent, and once it's healed, you can take out the jewelry whenever you want.

Choose a piercing. Pick a spot that you can easily keep clean and that you're keen to accessorize. It's likely to be a part of your body that's frequently visible when you're going about your day. Nostril and septum piercings are popular choices, as are all varieties of ear piercing.

Pay up. Piercing service will likely cost you at least fifty bucks, not counting any jewelry you buy. Pricing will vary based on location of piercing, size, and type of jewelry.

Follow instructions. You should receive guidelines on proper aftercare. Clean your piercing regularly. Infections are gross and not fun to deal with.

DO NOT DIY!

You might have a friend who claims that they can do your new piercing for free with only a sewing needle and a potato. Do not, under any circumstances, take them up on this offer. Piercers train for years on the proper hygiene and technique for their craft. If you're not careful, you can end up with a nasty infection. It's much safer to cough up the money and get your piercing done professionally.

95 Get an Astrology Reading

Stargazers have been drawing comparisons between the movement of celestial bodies and events on Earth for eons. They've attempted to explain the mysteries of life linking the position of the planets to birthdays and personal fates. Every star sign has its own mythology, characteristics, and symbolic animal or archetype—Capricorns are goal-oriented goats, Tauruses are headstrong bulls, Aquariuses are idealistic water bearers, and so on.

Ultra-rational types dismiss horoscopes as pseudoscientific nonsense, while diehard enthusiasts won't make a move without consulting their star chart. Even if you're not a believer, astrology can be a fun tool for self-reflection.

How to Do It

Sign in. Thousands of apps and websites offer daily horoscope readings. Give one of these a try. Enter your exact date and time of birth, and read what it has to say about your unique cosmological position.

Make an appointment. Check online to find an astrologer near you, or sign up for a digital consultation. During your meeting, the astrologer will ask when you were born, plus some questions about your family, social life, and goals. Based on this info, they'll create a customized astrological chart for you. The chart is a big circle with lots of lines running through it. Its southern hemisphere relates to your external life, while the northern hemisphere deals with your inner life. The circle is divided into twelve signs of the zodiac, each linked to traits, parts of your identity, and aspects of your daily existence. As the astrologer fills in and interprets your chart for you, feel free to ask specific questions.

Employ a grain of salt. If you're not happy with the answers you get, remember that astrology is all about interpretation. Take whatever resonates to heart and forget the rest—or reimagine a meaning that feels more fitting.

CARDS ON THE TABLE

Tarot is another fun way to interpret symbols and extract meaning from an unscientific source. Tarot cards became linked with fortune-telling in seventeenth-century France. After shuffling and picking a few cards from the deck, a reader can decipher how business, love, money, and spirituality impact your life. Don't let the death card scare you—it often simply means the end of some aspect of your life, perhaps a bad habit or relationship. Tarot decks come in a vast variety of designs, so an enthusiast may decide to invest in one (or more) with a distinctive aesthetic.

96 Build a Bonfire

Fire is a mysterious, powerful, and creative yet potentially destructive force of nature. Many cultures celebrate holidays by building fires. A bonfire can be a social gathering point, can keep you warm on a cold camping trip, or can bask a potential date in a romantic glow. Building a fire of your own will fill you with the warmth of accomplishment and can be a fun bonding activity for friends.

How to Do It

Gather with a group. Include some outdoorsy people! Older family members or ex-Boy Scouts usually have some fire-building experience.

Find a spot. You should be at least 60 feet (18 m) away from anything that might be flammable. You don't want your small blaze to get out of control.

Bring supplies. You'll need kindling, like twigs and branches, as well as big pieces of wood up to 6 feet (1.8 m) long and 5 inches (13 cm) around. Wood should be dry but not rotted. (That dead tree your friend's dad cut down last week will need another year or so to dry out properly.) Bring more wood than you think you'll need. It's easy to underestimate the amount necessary to get a good blaze going. Bales of straw work too. Also bring a shovel, rake, or other tool that you can use to stoke and control the flames. Make sure plenty of water is handy and, if possible, bring a fire extinguisher.

Start the blaze. Gather the kindling in a teepee formation about 4 feet (1.2 m) high and around. Carefully light the kindling with paper and a lighter or long match. As the fire begins to burn, add more kindling and wood, slowly graduating to larger pieces. With proper maintenance, the bonfire should burn for a couple of hours. Dowse whatever's left before you leave.

DON'T PLAY WITH FIRE

If you're undertaking the task of building a fire, you must also undertake the responsibility of being safe about it. That means following these rules:

- Don't build a bonfire on a windy day or evening.
- If the wind suddenly picks up while the fire is burning, keep a close eye on your flames, and extinguish them immediately if your fire starts to spread in any direction.
- Don't add flammable liquids, fireworks, aerosols, or batteries.
- Don't leave the fire unattended.
- *Never* leave a fire still burning. Use water, dirt, and extinguishers to put it all the way out, and scatter the embers so they won't relight.

Uncontrolled fire can wreak havoc on an area and destroy people's lives. Protect yourself from a potential criminal conviction and protect your community from danger by always practicing proper fire safety.

97 Watch the Sunrise

So many things in life are completely unpredictable, but there's one thing you can bet on without fail: The sun sets in the west and rises in the east. Since the sun sets in the evening, we're often around to watch it sink westward in a display of vibrant colors. Watching it rise from the east is more challenging, since we're often asleep when it happens. But witnessing a sunrise is an awesome, beautiful, and humbling experience. Sacrifice sleeping in for at least one morning to watch the sun soar into the sky and light up the planet.

How to Do It

Time it right. Check a weather website or app for the exact time of the sunrise, which varies slightly from day to day. Set your alarm for at least an hour before the scheduled time so you won't miss it. (And set some backup alarms in case you fall back asleep.)

Get in position. If possible, head to a broad, flat landscape—ideally out in nature—where nothing will get in the way of your view. Or scramble up to the peak of a hill or small mountain for a bird's-eye view. Check in advance if your location of choice will have an unobstructed eastern view. You don't want to arrive only to discover a billboard has been erected directly in your sight line.

Unplug. Resist the temptation to take a ton of pictures during the sunrise. They never look nearly as good as the real thing, and it's more special to fully experience the dawning of the day without worrying if the flash is set to Auto. Spend a few moments contemplating the great big universe and your place in it as you gaze in wonder at this star, shining at you from 93 million miles away.

QUITE THE SIGHT

Solar eclipses, when the moon blocks sunlight by coming directly between Earth and the sun, are rare but truly spectacular. When they do occur, they usually draw huge crowds. Read up on their infrequent appearances and see if you can be in the right place at the right time to view an obscuring of the sun. Just don't look directly at the eclipse! The sun's rays can still damage your vision from behind the moon. View it instead through special glasses made for the occasion.

98 Spend a Day in Silence

Are you tired of the constant noise of the world? With twenty-four-hour news cycles and constantly refreshing social media feeds, it can be hard to keep your head on straight. Try devoting an entire day to maximum quiet. Temporarily escaping the usual cacophony of voices, advertisements, and bass-boosted music can help you feel centered, giving you a chance to process thoughts and feelings you've had trouble pinning down. Or it can be a way to let go of your thoughts and let your mind rest. See if you can get through a whole day without even talking. Afterward, you may find that you're much more conscious of the words you say—and much more appreciative of precious moments of silence.

How to Do It

Lay groundwork. Pick a day when you won't be required to speak for school or work. Let your friends and relatives know ahead of time that you'll be unusually quiet and ask them to respect your silence and privacy throughout the day.

Find a relaxing environment. If that's not your home, hunker down in the middle of a tranquil park for the afternoon. A quiet gallery in a big museum or a corner of a chill coffee shop can work if outdoor options are off the table.

Soothe yourself. Spend the day reading and meditating, *not* scrolling on your phone. Focus on sounds that are usually obscured by noise pollution or your own yapping, such as the chirping of birds or the crashing of waves. Put some headphones on and listen to gentle music. If you must communicate with others, use a sign language or write notes.

RETREAT INTO SILENCE

Some meditation centers and monasteries offer silent retreats that can last from one day to two months, with only very short periods of conversation allowed. If these aren't viable options, consider spending a weekend hanging out with a few like-minded friends in a DIY mini-retreat.

99 Bury a Time Capsule

It may sound weird, but people have been burying time capsules—collections of important items that represent particular people and time periods—for millennia. In many cultures, people were buried with items that represented who they were and how they spent their time on this planet. But you don't have to shuffle off this mortal coil to gather a few meaningful possessions and hide them away for posterity. Years from now you can dig them up yourself, while still alive and kicking, as a reminder of what was important to you when you were younger.

How to Do It

Vet the treasures. Select a few items you want to preserve. You can also get friends to contribute. That'll diversify the collection and bring you all back together years later for the unearthing. Pick items that matter to you and represent your time and place—but that you can bear to part with!

Bury the treasures. Put everything in a sturdy, airtight box, ideally made of metal, and bury it. Where? If your family owns a home with a backyard, ask if you can dig a hole in an unused plot of dirt. If not, a neighbor or close friend might let you shovel out a portion of their yard. Way out in the woods can work too. Just be sure not to upset any wildlife or leave a mess. Plant a marker near the buried capsule so you'll remember where to find it and store a map with the location of your time capsule in a safe place.

Leave the treasures. Though your teenage years may seem like a real mixed bag, this is still a unique time in your life. Deciding what goes into your time capsule gives you an excuse to take note of what's important to you—and what you're ready to let go. Years later, when you find these things again, you'll be grateful for the prearranged trip down memory lane. And if you never do dig it up yourself, think how cool it would be for someone from the future to find it thousands of years from now and wonder what a Wii remote is.

WHAT YOU LEAVE BEHIND

Your time capsule should contain items that spark joy but that you won't miss on a day-to-day basis over the next decade or so. Here are some examples:

- a copy of a favorite book
- a stone or shell from the beach
- printouts of favorite photos
- a broken video game controller

If you've made it this far, you might be thinking, "I'll never have time to do all the things I want to do before I finish high school." That's okay! You don't have to tackle everything right this second. Just follow your gut and start somewhere. You might even decide to try a project or adventure that we haven't covered at all! It's not about checking off boxes; it's about discovering a little bit more about yourself and the world. By the time graduation rolls around, you'll know that you've made the most of this stage of your life—and that you're ready to jump headfirst into whatever comes next.